Count It As a Vegetable . . . And

Move On!

Ending the Food-Abuse/Self-Abuse Cycle Of the Typical Dieter

by
Dolly Cowen, M.A.
&
Lynne Goldklang, M.A.

The Nurturing Connection
Agoura Hills, California
in conjunction with:
Isaac Nathan Publishing Co., Inc.
Woodland Hills, California

Library of Congress Cataloging-in-Publication Data

Cowen, Dolly
Goldklang, Lynne
 Count It As a Vegetable, and Move On: Ending the Food-Abuse/
 Self- Abuse Cycle of the Typical Dieter
 1. Diet 2. Health 3. Addiction 4. Self-Help

ISBN 0-914615-30-0

Library of Congress Catalog Card Number: 2001-132815

Manufactured in the United States of America

First Edition, August, 2001
Second Edition, January, 2002

Published by:
 The Nuturing Connection
 5923 Kanan Road
 Agoura Hills, CA 91301
 (818) 725-3125

In conjunction with:
 Isaac Nathan Publishing Co., Inc.
 22711 Cass Avenue
 Woodland Hills, CA 91364
 (818) 225-9631

Contents

This book is dedicated to our families with much love:
Alan, Aron, Robby and Kate Cowen.
Don, Rob and Jessica Goldklang.
Carol, Josh, Jacob and Alice Greenstein.

Thanks to Carol Greenstein
and Aron Cowen for the artwork.

Introduction

If you have ever struggled with your weight or eating habits, this book is for you.

This isn't just another weight loss book. It's not about loss at all. It is about gaining self-respect as you take back your life from the emotional wasteland of the food-abuse/self-abuse cycle.

Both of us have spent over twenty years working with people who have come to us to lose weight. We know from our experience as psychotherapists and teachers that the journey is not about finding the perfect diet. We understand crazy eating and crazier dieting because we lived it, falsely believing that gaining and losing weight was about miracle cures, supreme willpower or destiny.

We have learned from our lives and work that going from chaos to peace in a world obsessed with eating and dieting is a process of living well, not a product measured in pounds of flesh. It is a way off the treadmill of yo-yo eating so you no longer have to feel like a caged rat running endlessly, waiting for the whirling to stop.

It is about a "Circle of Health," a holistic way of eating and living that can bring about permanent weight loss in ways that are life affirming.

There are three sections. The first— *Count It as a Vegetable and Move On*—is about handling emotional eating and making behavior changes.

The second—***How to Lose Weight and Keep It Off***—presents a holistic plan for permanent weight loss.

The third section—***Our Stories***—is about our personal stories. We want you to know us and understand that we have lived what we write.

We invite you to sit back, relax, read and reread the book in any order you choose until the words go from head to heart. Our mission is to guide you into the deepest reaches of yourself so that you can transcend the food-abuse/self-abuse cycle and emerge changed from the inside out.

> *Dolly Cowen*
> *Lynne Goldklang*
> *January, 2002*

SECTION ONE:
COUNT IT AS A VEGETABLE
AND MOVE ON

This is Dolly's section. Both of us have contributed to the content but we are presenting the chapters in Dolly's voice so you can feel like a participant in her meetings.

This section is all about the emotional connection to eating. Each chapter deals with an important life issue that impacts both weight and self-image.

You will be able to make changes in the present from the vantage point of greater understanding of your past and empathy for your journey toward a better quality of life.

COUNT IT AS A VEGETABLE

AND MOVE ON

"Count it as a vegetable and move on" started at one of my Weight Watcher™ meetings. Annie, one of my most dedicated members, was very upset because she had gained two pounds after six months of consistent weight loss. She was desperate:

> Dolly, I want to quit. I binged all weekend after all these months of being good. I even ate a whole cheesecake. How can I fix this? How can I count it? I feel like a failure.

I understood her frustration and longing to fix. That used to be me. I would eat something "fattening" and tell myself I was a bad person. I'd go on a deprivation diet in an attempt to punish myself and undo the damage quickly. This kind of "fixing" led to self-contempt and giving up. I didn't want this to happen to Annie and struggled to find the words that would reach her.

"Look Annie, you're human. So you ate a whole cheesecake. There is no way to fix it and no way to count it unless you want to count it as all your fats for a year. Why don't you just pretend that the whole binge, cheesecake and all, was vegetables. Just **count it as a vegetable and move on**."

She laughed and agreed to ease up on herself and get back on the program that worked so well for her. She went into the meeting room and told the rest of the group about her new mantra. By the time I came in to start the lecture, it was a hot topic of discussion.

It didn't end with that meeting. People kept coming back week after week with examples of how they were using "Count it as a vegetable" to live with themselves in a better way.

I believe it touched so many people because we are longing for a way to stop our continual character assassination. We want to be more compassionate with ourselves but don't know how.

"Count it as a vegetable" goes way beyond food issues. It is more than a technique to deal with minor incidents in life. There is always an underlying deeper issue when we turn against ourselves.

Randi, a woman in one of my meetings described the "disaster" that occurred as she was ready to leave for work:

I was racing through the house doing a million things when I threw on my clothes and noticed that my slacks were full of electricity. I ran into the kitchen and sprayed myself with Static Cling when suddenly I sensed that something was very wrong. I took a good look at the container in my hand and saw that in my haste I had grabbed a can of cooking spray and now had an oil slick all over me and the floor.

I wanted to laugh at myself but all I could feel was fury at my stupidity. I knew my self-contempt was undeserved but couldn't stop the inner tirade. What I needed to do was clean up and move on. What I actually did was change clothes and grab a brownie to soothe my feelings instead of a mop to clean the floor. I came home to that slimy mess at the end of a long workday.

We talked about the incident in class and it became clear that Randi's reaction had nothing to do with the spray mix-up. The real issue was her unrealistic desire to be a person who would never make that kind of mistake. Her image of herself as superwoman— in charge and in control—was badly damaged.

As we talked, Randi recognized that the eating and beating herself up did nothing to eliminate the mess or give her what she really wanted—protection against making those kinds of careless mistakes in the future.

We resist softening our inner dialogue even though it feels so good to treat ourselves with respect. We are afraid we will do nothing and be nothing if we drive ourselves with a steering wheel instead of a whip. It takes deep work to be self-forgiving and to move on.

That inside voice goes back to childhood. Many of us were raised with punitive parents who may have loved us but believed that children learn best through blaming and shaming. They were not quick to forgive. They wanted us to learn from what happened so we wouldn't do it again.

My parents were in the Holocaust and survived an environment where a mistake could mean death. They were hard on my brother and me because that was the only way they knew to keep us safe.

We continue the parenting we grew up with through our inner talk. There is something about the guilt and shame that feels necessary. We are living out that old tape that says: "I'll teach you a lesson you'll never forget." If we just forgive ourselves easily then we think we won't learn anything. We believe that we have to parent ourselves in the way it was done to us.

We get confused about the use of self-power. If we attack ourselves over the oil slick or the eating binge or some other mistake, we can be powerful in our anger and get a momentary high from the adrenaline rush. When I turn against myself, I have the illusion that I am doing something about the situation even though I'm just wallowing in the feelings of self-contempt. The punitive inner dialogue saps the energy needed to move forward.

A friend has a slogan hanging in her office that says: "I don't worry much about tomorrow but I keep hoping yesterday will get better." As long as we are busy attacking ourselves, we get to stay in the fantasy that we can redo the past.

Each of us may look like a grown-up to the rest of the world but inside we are the two-year-old who cries when the vacuum cleaner goes on and shouts "NO" all day with only minor impact on those big people making all the decisions. We long for control over everything from the cheesecake to the earthquake. We get disillusioned when we find we can't even control ourselves—at least, not without ongoing work.

Control is a very big issue. I see over four hundred people a week in my meetings and the discussion often turns to handling setbacks and poor choices—those times when we feel "out of control." We were talking about what really goes on at a deep level when we get ballistic over our mistakes. The gut-wrenching reaction for most of my members is major disappointment that turns to self-outrage. We reflexibly fight against any relief that would come from being gentler with ourselves because of the voice inside proclaiming: "You should have known better."

Many of us grew up believing that when we made a mistake we were bad. Little infractions often felt like sins. "I'm ashamed of you" was used for the "B" on a report card or a missed catch on the playing field.

We were often in trouble just for being young and inexperienced. Our little hands would drop the full glass of milk. We would forget to wipe off the muddy shoes before walking in the house. We would leave the toys on the floor and want to watch TV when it was time for homework. A gentler approach with ourselves forces us to abandon old tapes that contain messages that have been with us forever. Shutting off those familiar tapes can feel like killing off our parents, teachers and all the other big people that were part of our childhood world.

The message many of us got was "I can't trust you to behave right." Now when we have an instinct about what is good or bad in our lives whether it be a food or a job or a person, it is easy to discount that inner message with: "What do you know? Why should I listen to you, anyway. You're not trustworthy." We make decisions about feeding friends or family members but we turn to "experts" to tell us what to eat. We often feel self-contempt because we turned away from our own inner knowing.

Some of my group members had parents who would stay mad for the whole day but would be over it by morning so that when everyone woke up life was back to normal. They felt exonerated as if they had a clean slate. Many of us are good at taking a tiny mistake and letting it ruin the whole day so we can have the feeling of being pure and fresh when the sun rises on the new morn. We binge today and hope for a tomorrow when we will be the perfect "dieter."

The process of embracing "count it as a vegetable and move on" starts by grieving those places inside us where we still feel wounded. It is very hard to get to the "moving on" without feeling the pain of accepting that whatever has happened is a done deal and there's nothing we can do about it. Until we let go of our yesterdays, we are still trying to control what happened. We are going back to the past, trying to make it different. If we can bring back the flawed moment, we will have another chance. Letting go is accepting that there are no more chances with that particular circumstance. We will have new opportunities but not with the one that has past. It's really over.

A man in one of my groups was furious with himself because he lost ten thousand dollars on a computer transaction. The money loss was a big financial blow and he believed that he let his family down. It had been over a month and he was still ruminating over the crisis. His weight went up and his mood continued to spiral down.

His wife did everything she could to be a source of comfort to him. She even drove him to the beach and they walked along the ocean and watched the waves on a beautiful Southern California day. It didn't help. He was still overwhelmed by guilt, beating himself up without mercy.

Finally, his wife was done with compassion and turned to him, shouting: "Enough already. I don't care how much money it is or what a jerk you think you are. I want you to count it as a vegetable and move on! "

He was shocked but got the message and finally let go of the negative energy and began dealing with his grief. He sobbed and let himself mourn not only the lost money but also the death of the illusion that he could never make that kind of mistake. It wasn't easy but when he let go of the self-contempt and grieved, he was able to move on to begin the process of recouping financially. When he released the self-hatred he also stopped using food as an emotional pain killer.

He was fortunate to have a loving wife who encouraged him to be self-forgiving. We may be ready to "count it as a vegetable" but people we care about may not be as supportive as we would wish when it comes to our human foibles.

The other day I filled up my gas tank, paid at the pump and began to drive off when I heard this huge noise. I looked around and saw the man from the station wildly waving his arms and screaming for me to stop. It was then that I realized I had driven off with the gas pump attached to my car.

Of course, I was horrified as I saw the damage to the pump and my car. I knew the insurance would take care of the expenses but I was still shaken up. However, by the time I headed for home, I was fine with myself and hysterically laughing over the whole incident. It was truly an "I Love Lucy" moment in life.

I got home and talked to some of my friends. They couldn't stop laughing at the image of me driving away connected to the gas pump. Then my husband Alan came home. Alan is a good man who spent years as Chief of Paramedic Services for Los Angeles. In his work, a mistake could cost lives. He also is a guy who loves his car like it was part of the family.

In spite of everything I knew about my Alan, I still expected him to hear my story and laugh, saying to me: "That's the funniest thing I ever heard. That's my honey. You're so adorable. I just love that about you—those funny little things you do."

What he actually said was: "You did what? I've never in my life heard of anyone doing such a crazy thing. How could you have let that happen? I just can't believe it."

Now I no longer felt okay about myself. I felt shame and wished I could disappear. My stomach was in knots and I wanted to either eat or start an argument with Alan. Instead I sat down and just let myself feel the disappointment for a few minutes.

The "grieving" was not about what happened at the gas station but about my sorrow that I would never have unconditional love from my husband or from anyone. I also had to grieve that I no longer was going to ease my emotional pain by eating. It took all my strength but I was able to get up and go on with the day without dragging the incident around just like I did the pump.

"Count it as a vegetable" is a vivid affirmation that we can go on whether we are dealing with small mistakes of the moment or big issues from the past. Just becoming aware of the concept can start the process of being kinder to ourselves. It is a concept that moves steadily from head to heart. It doesn't prevent emotional pain nor does it exonerate us from the damage we have done to ourselves or others. The spilled milk, broken objects, hasty words and other actions have consequences that still need attention. We need a tool to stop the energy drain of trying to undo the past and be perfect in the present. We need a reminder that pencils have erasers, computers have a delete button and human beings will continue to be human.

"Count is as a vegetable and move on" is both a tool for future progress and a light-hearted reminder of our membership in the human, not superhuman, species.

Buried Bones
And Other Pacifiers

I was five years old, riding my trike around the apartment, giggling as I circled about in my little play area, totally unaware that my dad was in one of his dark moods. Suddenly he jumped up from his chair, grabbed me off my tricycle and hurled it out the window.

I never forgot that incident. His fury struck without warning. I was terrified and said nothing. I held in my tears and tiptoed into the kitchen to find my mother. She sat with me as we ate cookies together. They were all warm and melty, fresh out of the oven. I sighed with relief and ate until my stomach hurt.

I made the mistake of asking my dad in recent years if he remembered that day, hoping he would finally express remorse. His response was bewilderment. "What's the big deal, Dolly. I had a hard day at work and couldn't stand the noise. It was just a toy."

A few months after that brief conversation, my dad died. Along with accepting that he is gone, I must also give up the fantasy that someday he would come to me, hold me close and tell me how sorry he was for all the times his misdirected anger came my way.

The grown-up me understands and appreciates how difficult living must have been for my parents after losing so many family members in the Holocaust. They took care of me physically but couldn't emotionally. In our home, food was the soother for painful feelings.

Food feels so good in the moment that we don't want the pleasure to end. Deep inside, we know the aftermath of emotional eating will be agony but we turn away from that inner knowing because of our need for the instant relief food provides.

I remember watching my dog digging up an old bone. We have a drawer full of new bones but that wasn't what he wanted. He plowed deeper and deeper into the earth, paws working frantically until finally he uncovered an old muddy bone. He put it in his mouth, didn't chew it, just let it sit there on his tongue as he dozed contentedly in the sun.

I believe he buries bones so he can call on them as needed. He doesn't trust that there will always be enough fresh bones for him. He is like the baby who falls asleep with a breast in his mouth or the toddler clutching her favorite blanket.

I like to observe young children because they are so connected to what they need in the moment. I was at the car wash and noticed a little one about eighteen months old in a stroller clutching his bottle. He looked up at his mom and started gurgling and cooing— trying to engage her. She was staring in space, preoccupied and paid no attention to the baby.

He started to fuss but she didn't even glance in his direction. He took his bottle and threw it on the ground. She picked up the bottle and gave it to him without a word or any eye contact. He threw his bottle down again and she picked it up and said to him, "Come on now, you know how to hold a bottle." She still was looking out in space as she mechanically gave him the bottle once again.

He continued trying to engage her but there was nothing. He started whimpering but she still did not respond. Finally, he stopped and turned into himself and started sucking his thumb.

He seemed to be in a lot of sorrow—almost despair—as he curled up into a fetus-like ball—as if he were saying, " I give up. I'll find a way to comfort myself." It was as though he suddenly felt his aloneness and turned inward to grieve.

It broke my heart to witness the sorrow of this little guy. I hoped that what I was observing was not typical of his interaction with this self-absorbed woman who was either his mother or a significant caretaker. This time the baby sucked his thumb but I wondered what it might be in the future. Would he turn to food, alcohol, drugs or the socially sanctioned outlets like people pleasing or workaholism to deal with his bottomless grief?

We often feel like that baby and want to be held and comforted. When it doesn't happen from the outside, we no longer curl up with our blanket or suck our thumb. For those of us who are eaters, we turn to food as the closest we can come to a womb-like experience.

When we use food to soothe us, the food becomes a conditioned stimulus for good feelings. The sight, thought or smell of food is like the sound of a can opener for a hungry animal. A sense of positive anticipation grows as we await our "fix". What we need is to find non-food cues to elicit good feelings and ease our anxiety.

When I would walk into the house after a long day working, the house was a cue to eat as I quickly greeted my family then ran into the kitchen and threw open the refrigerator door. I had years of associations where home and food meant refuge from the outside world. Even if my day was totally pleasant, I still needed food to feel relaxed in the transition from work to home.

A few years ago I decided to undo years of conditioning and learn to unwind by submerging myself in water instead of food.

Today when I come home after work, I race into the house, kiss anyone who is home, hug the dogs, greet the bird, throw off my clothes and jump into the tub. I let the hot soapy water and fragrant oil fill my senses as I sit there and soak for about twenty minutes. I emerge calm, relaxed, ready to be with family and handle the millions of errands calling to me from every room of the house.

This way of soothing is second nature to me today but the first time I tried to relax in a bath was a disaster. I was a five minute shower person and felt guilty about engaging in tub indulgence. All I could think about in the water was what I would be making for dinner. I couldn't get the bubbles to foam the way I wanted so the water felt murky not bubbly. My "old enough to wait kids" were knocking at the bathroom door with questions every other minute. I exited the bathtub much more stressed than when I entered.

It takes some trial and error to get the hang of non-food ways to relax. However, it doesn't take long before the bubble bath from hell becomes heavenly or a nature walk moves from exhaustion to exhilaration. The bigger issue involved in finding non-food soothers is believing that we are worth the time and effort required to really take care of ourselves.

When we were very young we knew instinctively what we needed. I was at the grocery store baby watching again. The couple in line ahead of me had a toddler who was standing in a grocery cart that was loaded with stuff—soda cans, produce, cereal boxes and a big package with several rolls of paper towels. It was very crowded and chaotic at the store.

In the midst of all the commotion, this little one took the blanket she was holding, spread it out over the merchandise and put her cheek on the section of blanket that was over the soft paper towels. She sighed contentedly and started to fall asleep.

Her mother and father did not want her napping as they were about to leave the store so they took away the blanket saying "no, no" and stood her back up in the cart.

The little girl grabbed the blanket back again, spread it out on the groceries and lay down once again with her head on the paper towels. This time the parents smiled at each other and decided that "baby knows best."

It was an example of the child telling the parents: "I'm tired. Let me sleep. And if you can't provide a way for me to nap then I'm going to find it myself."

The parents ignored the baby's cues the first time because of their own needs. The shopping excursion was probably during their daughter's nap time. The complexities of parental schedules are often in conflict with a child's needs. The young baby will eat, sleep, play, fuss and live by instincts. If parents constantly divert the baby's needs in favor of their own, the growing child will soon lose the ability to listen to inner signals.

Parents must socialize their children and teach them how to function in a world that isn't designed just for them. Unfortunately, the process of doing that is often too severe and most of us quickly lose contact with our instincts.

There was a time when the emotional eater knew about physical hunger cues and didn't want a bottle to satisfy needs for rest or activity or love. For those of us who are eaters, food slowly began to be the main pacifier for everything. As I watch babies, I see up close how the longing we have for perfect attunement with another comes from those early experiences when our parents may have loved us and provided for us physically but not emotionally.

A recent magazine article talked about a method for helping premature babies thrive faster called "kangaroo care." The fragile baby, tubes and all, is placed on top of a parent for hours at a time—skin touching skin. Sometimes the parent's shirt actually serves as a real pouch. This intimate process of joining with the parent has increased overall survival rates of these babies. They start to thrive by gaining weight rapidly and are able to leave the hospital sooner than premature infants under traditional care.

We long for that kind of deep connection with another all our lives. If our basic needs for emotional as well as physical care were met when we were growing up, it is easier for us to deal with the stresses of our adult lives. We need to learn how to handle adversity when we are young, but not at a level that breaks the spirit.

Finding non-food ways to cope is vital to our well-being. Sometimes our non-food soothers are things we do to feel better. Other times it might be an image, sound or smell that takes us back to a memory.

My friend and co-author Lynne describes how she used imagery as a way to grieve for her mother:

My much loved mother died a few years ago in her nineties. I was recently in a drugstore that had been a favorite spot for an outing in the last year of her life. We had this routine where we would go to the ice cream counter and my mom would buy a double-scoop cone. Ice cream was her passion. She knew I didn't want one but would insist that I take the first bite of her cone. Then she would sit contentedly eating and people watching while I did the shopping.

I love sweets but ice cream does nothing for me yet I found myself pulled to the ice cream counter as if by some magnetic force, emerging with a huge cone overflowing with my mother's two favorite flavors. I sat down on "her" bench and tried to capture something but all I felt was emptiness along with a chill as the cold ice cream trickled down my insides.

I threw away the half-eaten cone and went back to the bench and just sat and thought about my mother. I pictured her sitting on this same spot smiling, enjoying her treat and striking up a conversation with anyone who greeted her. Lots of people used to stop and say hello to the twinkling little lady with the big ice cream cone.

The sadness evoked by these images was worth experiencing because I felt the comfort of my mother's presence as I sat with my memories. I left the drugstore filled with something that ice cream could never give me.

Maria, a member of one of my meetings, told our group a powerful example of how images can be cruel or comforting. She told us her story:

I was in a horrible car accident where a drunk driver hit my car. The car was demolished and I was bruised and scratched. The driver was propelled out of his car and landed right on top of my hood. These images from the accident were torturing me and the only way I could get relief was by hanging out in front of the refrigerator. I was eating my way into oblivion and desperately wanted to stop.

Finally, I came up with a plan. Whenever a memory of the driver came into my mind, I would replace it with the sweet face of my beloved grandson. The image of that baby always brought immense pleasure. Within a week, I had totally stopped picturing scenes from the accident. I ended up gaining self-respect not weight.

As she talked, we could see her face light up with joy when she mentioned her grandson. For Maria, the baby is a powerful positive cue that always elicits good feelings. It is her favorite "buried bone" that she can call upon when needed.

Images, memories, and objects can be used as healthy pacifiers. My neighbor has a wonderful music box collection. Her favorite is the one that her husband gave her on her fortieth birthday. It plays "Younger Than Springtime". Whenever she opens that box and hears the tinkling notes, she feels good.

My husband jumps on his motorcycle and soars down the road feeling his stress blow away with the wind against his face.

When I was little and upset, my parents didn't say: "Let's talk about it, draw about it, play some music, take a bubble bath, go for a walk, have lots of hugs." They did what they knew to do--suppress my reactions or offer cookies. The task of finding healthy ways to deal with my feelings is one I had to learn on my own as an adult.

Food always fixes my wounds but never for long and when they open up again, the cut is deeper and more painful.

One of the healthier ways I comfort myself is to curl up in my favorite chair with pen and notebook. I write and cry and cry and write until everything is out. After years of stuffing feelings with food, it feels so freeing to express, not repress. Sometimes I save what has been written, other times tear it up and scatter the pieces. I feel cleansed when finished. Then like my dog and his bone, I'm at ease.

Whenever we want to calm a baby, we instinctively talk softly and caress the baby, cooing, singing or speaking in soothing tones. We need to do the same for ourselves. We can softly stroke our faces and tell ourselves it will be okay. Often we turn outside to food because we can't get any nurturance inside from ourselves.

There isn't any one pacifier that always works and sometimes the habit of grabbing a food fix overpowers a more healthy response. We can be gentle with ourselves when that happens. Non-food pacifiers sometimes get lost in an emotional storm. We are locked in what feels like a struggle with an inner devil—an alien part of us—who beckons to us with treats, promising to make the moment sweet in exchange for an aftermath of a bitter tomorrow.

I was a stress eater for most of my life and when any little thing bothers me, I automatically want to reach for food. I crave the immediate pay-off. Food is easy to get and can send us into states of ecstasy in the moment. It is easy to forget about the moment after.

I've learned to tell the difference between a true stress reliever and a false deceiver. It is very simple. If the soother has a negative after effect, then it is not the real thing. The box of candy might taste great going down but a moment later the stress returns along with additional stress over the potential consequences of eating all that fat. Candy is a false lover who comes with sweet promises that always turn to pain.

We don't have to be the raging father who throws trikes out the window or the indulging mother who uses cookies as bandages for the heart. It takes effort but we can find our own way to dig bones and sleep on the soft grass with the sun shining down upon us.

💻 PC is Not a Personal Computer

In my world PC means portion control, a kind of personal computing that's done by mouth, not mouse.

Sometimes I wish I had a computer chip instead of a chocolate chip right in the heart of my hunger, controlling my wanting without any effort on my part. In spite of the wonders of human science, there is no technology that can make us stop eating at that optimum point just before a portion becomes a poison.

Portion control is about the emotional connection to eating that makes it so hard to separate from a feeding. It is also about the opportunity for personal triumph that comes when we stop using food as a drug and find healthy ways to take care of our deepest hungers.

Let's observe little Cindy, my neighbor's three year old. It's her first day of preschool. Her face is flushed with excitement as mom drives her toward the school. Cindy is gripping a lunch pail in one hand and teddy in the other. Teddy is an old baby toy that has lost most of its stuffing. Cindy sucks on teddy's ear like it was an infant pacifier.

When they arrive at the school, my neighbor takes her little girl out of the car seat. "Okay, honey, here we are. Leave teddy with me and he'll be waiting for you when I pick you up." Cindy gets teary as she slowly gets out of the car. Then she stops, picks up her beloved toy and gives the ragged ear one last suck. She sighs and skips off with mom to a new adventure.

I can relate to that story. I know what it is to want the last suck. Deep within us is the memory of primal comfort from breast or bottle and panic can arise at even the thought of separation. When we feel strong emotionally, the parting is easier. An adult can hold the future in the present and know that the separation is not forever. There will be more food and ample moments of comfort.

When our world is rocky we feel like a baby at that moment of terror when mother has left the room for a few minutes. To the infant, out of sight means gone forever. Sometimes, we feel more like Cindy, a toddler, able to tolerate some separation from mom or dad or even teddy, but it is painful and we want to delay the moment of parting.

I order a small fries along with my low fat veggie burger. I take a few golden morsels from the plate. Now I am in food heaven but my plan is to eat just half a portion, so I ask the waiter to take the rest away. I grab two more fries as the plate is being removed and anxiously watch the food disappear from view.

I'm filled with wanting as I look around and see other people eating. The restaurant seems to be papered with giant mouths and flying hands stuffing unlimited amounts of huge greasy fries into skinny bodies. I'm jealous, deprived, distraught.

The pain lasts less than five minutes. Soon I'm back in my car, jazzed, listening to blaring music as I drive away relishing a sense of victory. I didn't win anything tangible yet the thrill of integrity is sweet and not at all greasy.

We want, we want, we want, we want. We are the crying baby, the whiny toddler, the greedy child, the rebellious teen, the adult who attempts to feed yesterday by gorging today.

We are feeding our history—all the food we didn't get, all the love we didn't get, all the wounds from years of deprivation. We never feel full when we are using food to feed the deep hungers that have nothing to do with physical need for food.

I love donuts but donuts hate me and just a few bites cause major stomach distress. My office is near a donut shop and I often stop there to get a cup of tea. I always want a donut and feel angst when the tea comes with nothing else, just a lonely tea bag and a cup of hot water. The grown-up part of me is content and not at all deprived by my choice but the little kid inside feels pain at every whim not instantly granted. I've learned the hard way to only go into that shop when the adult part of me is strong, not when I'm feeling little and vulnerable.

A few years back Alan and I drove our firstborn to college in a city far from home. This was a real separation. We knew he would never be our little boy again. It jarred me to realize that I wouldn't be picking him up after school that afternoon. I knew in my head that this was a good separation. Yet, I wept along with my husband as we said goodbye and supported our son as he began his journey toward manhood.

Let's go back to little Cindy. She left teddy and entered the world of preschool. What if preschool was a nightmare for her? What if I was still crying weeks after my son's departure for college? What if letting go of food means we are letting go of our only means of self-soothing and don't know what to do other than eat?

Portion control can jolt us from the comfort of a feeding into the pit of our colicky feelings that keep us restless and distressed. It may pull us into a void—a state of transition that is hard to bear. If the pieces of our lives that aren't about eating do not offer emotional sustenance, it will be a grueling struggle to separate from the immediate soothing of a food fix. We will remain the child who never wants to leave teddy for the big world.

Portion control is an opportunity for self-care and understanding at the deepest level as we come face to face with the reasons we use excess food as a drug to sooth or stimulate us.

As we walk around in a world mined with fabulous food where-ever we go, desire and temptation stalk us. We don't want to miss anything. There have been enough losses and slammed doors to our wants. It feels like a mini-death to say no to our food desires. Our food whims are so easy to fulfill, so much easier than our real wants.

I can be at dinner with my husband happily eating a small piece of cheesecake for dessert until I glance across the room and notice a man three tables away eating key lime pie. Suddenly the cheese-cake no longer tastes so good as I obsess about the pie and dream up schemes to get it.

I go out to breakfast with a friend and have a wonderful omelet. She orders oatmeal and I look at it so longingly that my friend offers me some. I end up with a small portion of her cereal while she wants none of my omelet because she is full.

It took psychological digging for me to understand why I was never calm inside, always wanting, feeling out of control, playing out my problems in the arena of food. I wondered why I never felt "full."

When I was little, it wasn't okay to want. If I came home from school and told my mom about the shiny new shoes my friend had, she lectured me with some version of, "Be happy with what you have. Don't be jealous because you have more than many people." She would be upset with me for even the tiniest of wantings.

As an adult, I understand the lesson in her message but as a little girl I experienced constant shame and believed I was bad for longing and yearning.

I watched a mother and her young daughter at the mall picking out a swimsuit from a bin filled with suits that were identical in style and price. The child pulled out one with butterflies and wanted to try it on. Her face was filled with delight at the colorful pattern. "No," said the mom, "this one with flowers is prettier. Try on this one."

*

The little girl was polite but tried to convince her mom to let her have the one she loved. The mom yanked her away from the suits shouting, "You ungrateful child. Now you will have nothing. We're going right home this instant. I'm so ashamed of you."

When my daughter was little and we would go to the mall, she would fall in love with something from every store. She wanted candles from the candle store, cookies from the food court, a toy from the children's store, a new outfit from the department store. I would echo her enthusiasm and validate her desires. "Yes, honey, it is a beautiful dress, a fun toy, a sweet smelling candle, delicious cookies."

Sometimes I would buy her one or two things she wanted and other times we were just looking. Saying no to her endless wants could be done easily in a loving manner, not through shaming and blaming.

On one of her birthdays several years ago, my husband and sons were out of town so the two of us spent a whole day together celebrating. We went to a mega-toy store where Katie picked out an expensive stuffed animal; then we went to a sushi bar followed by a movie with lots of popcorn. We even stopped at a beauty salon and Katie had her first manicure.

After this long indulgent day, we were headed home when I stopped at the grocery store to pick up a few things. My tired and satiated child asked me for a quarter to put into the gumball machine.

I said, "No, Katie. Nothing more today." She started whining that it was just a quarter. I said, "No, I have our groceries and it's time to go home."

She cried as we left the store without the gumballs. My mother would have been furious and said something like: "It's never enough with you. If I give you a hand, you want the whole arm. You are never satisfied. You are just a spoiled brat."

I was never a spoiled brat and neither was my daughter. She was just ltired and overstimulated. "Katie," I said. "I know it's hard to end such a fun day. It is hard to stop when everything feels so good." As I mirrored what she felt, she immediately calmed down. It wasn't about the gumballs. It was about that young primitive endless wanting that goes way beyond what we need.

Today my teenaged Katie is very respectful of the rules of the household and is much more into giving than getting. She isn't burdened by years of feeling shame for the normal yearnings that are part of being a child. She isn't using food, as I did, in a futile attempt to heal deep wounds of wanting and not getting.

However, life isn't easy for Katie. There are lots of temptations for a teenager besides food. The other day she asked, "Mom, what's it like to smoke? I see lots of kids doing it." We talked for awhile and I made it clear that she wasn't allowed to smoke.

"But Mom. I just want to try it once. I don't want to die without ever having tried a cigarette."

"Let me think about it, Katie. If I decide to let you try it, it will be one cigarette in front of Daddy and me."

Katie looked shocked. "No Mom, no. Say no to me." Katie pleaded.

I realized she really didn't want to smoke and counted on me to stop her. She does the same thing with scary violent movies. She begs to go with her friends and then is relieved when I say no. She wants to see what she can get away with while hoping I will protect her from herself. My no becomes a boundary that keeps her from going into dangerous territory. Most of the time she doesn't need me to handle the temptations but when she does, I'm there.

Many of us are rebellious adolescents or younger when it comes to food. We have times when we feel out of control, prisoners of our endless wanting. We long for a parent figure to protect us from ourselves so we don't have to suffer the consequences of reckless impulses.

I can easily get into excessive behavior whether it be about eating, buying, cleaning or working—whatever I'm doing when a mood state hits. It took a major personality overhaul to learn how to call upon the strong adult part of me to say no to my limitless wants so I could feel safe in my own company.

I make my life easier by not putting myself into situations that have no external boundaries. I no longer go to buffets. There is something about all that "free" food that brings out the beast in me.

I don't go on cruises where the food mentality is "anything goes." People are lined up at midnight for pickled herring, pizza and creme desserts. The cruise director announces that the typical traveler gains a pound a day. This is not my version of a dream trip.

I can't do Las Vegas. Everything is without boundaries. People are up all hours. The buffets are obscene. Drinks are cheap or free to the gambler. The hotels are lavish, the music blaring, the neon flashing and the stimulation is non-stop.

I want peace, calm, wild fun in manageable doses. The wanting inside is hard to contain when the outside environment is a circus. Many of my friends and students have no problem with buffets, cruises or Vegas-like places. They like having choices and can go for the wholesome ones that are plentiful in situations that offer everything. It is important that each of us understand what to embrace and what to avoid so we don't set ourselves up for disaster.

Sometimes we don't want to think about limits. We want to go to the party and eat everything. We zone out at the movies with a giant popcorn that comes with free refills. We eat the whole box of candy, devour a carton of ice cream, stay up all night and sleep all day. We are acting out, telling ourselves we must have this thrill right now.

When those "out of bounds" moods hit, it is time to stop, breathe, ask ourselves, "What's going on?" It is time to firmly tell ourselves, "No."

Here is a simple but powerful process that can be a lifeline when you are struggling with portion control. . . .

- Stop what you are doing and give yourself a five minute "time out." Separate physically from the food by leaving the room. Be loving not punishing with yourself as though you were a beloved child who is overstimulated and needs to wind down.

Take a few breaths, sprinkle some cool water on your face. Move around the house to release pent up energy from your body or go outdoors and take a short walk.

- After five minutes, give yourself an emotional pat on the back to acknowledge your efforts. Extend the time in more five minute segments until the urgency of the feelings have subsided.

- Keep encouraging yourself and validate any small successes as you use this process to deal with the overload of feelings that can lead to unwanted eating behavior. Keep working on this process even if your early efforts don't always pay off.

We also can use positive repetitive self-talk to handle emotional eating situations that come up over and over again. Almost every evening I must deal with the urge to go in and out of the kitchen—wanting a little something. I calm myself down with a dialogue that goes something like this:

"Dolly, the kitchen is closed. It will reopen in the morning for breakfast. It's time to put your mouth to bed."

Then I floss and brush my teeth, gargle with mouthwash and then, just like I did with my kids when they were little, I kiss my mouth goodnight, tuck it in and sing it to sleep.

My students always laugh at the "putting your mouth to bed image" but have found it to be very helpful. Compassionate humor helps us cut through our resistance to setting limits on our eating desires.

Think of yourself as a baby at birth. The baby is often swaddled, wrapped tightly in a blanket so that the little one feels safe, secure, protected. There will be times in the future to be unwrapped, moving about freely without holding. The baby will grow and need less swaddling time but all through life there will be those moments of vulnerability when there will be a need to be held close.

We can learn to be the loving parent to ourselves who knows when to swaddle and when to fling off the covers. We can learn to recognize when the little vulnerable one inside us needs protection from the dangers out in a big scary world.

If we live with constant deprivation our hungers will grow. We can easily mistake our appetite for living as appetite for eating. Portion control doesn't mean torturing ourselves by severe dieting. It does mean doing whatever is necessary to make eating just a portion of our lives, not our reason for getting up in the morning. Our true needs go beyond the next meal.

If we can say no to eating that doesn't serve our health and well being, we will have energy left to say yes to our nonfood appetites.

"I want to smoke and drink."

"I want to party all night and sleep all day."

"I want to quit my job and lie around watching TV in my pajamas."

"I want to win the lottery."

"I want a drop dead gorgeous body."

"I want a perfect mate and lots of adoring lovers too."

"I want the whole box of chocolates and I want it now."

Our wanting is without limits. Self-created boundaries are the barriers we erect so that we are not prisoners of our impulses and are able to reap the rewards of behavior that is in harmony with our deepest wants and goals.

Portion control is a wake-up call that challenges us to find real nourishment in the way we live so we can take food and leave food in a balance that is a life-enhancing flow of energy.

A Baby Step is Just A Leap of Faith

I always wanted to be a therapist but didn't know where to start. What I did know was how to put off my want by turning it into a can't. Can't was easy. Can't was familiar. Can't fed my doubts: How would I pay for school with two sons in college? When would I find the time to study? Was I smart enough? Was I too old? Can't kept me overwhelmed, unable to move. Miraculously, the desire to fulfill my destiny survived and not even food could stuff down the rising need to act on my dream.

One day I called a few schools and asked for catalogues. Then I sent away for applications. I chose a school, mailed the enrollment form and miracle of miracles was accepted for the fall semester.

I didn't get into the old panic over how can I do it, will I be able to study, will people like me, will I still be a good mother, will I, would I, could I . . . ? What I actually said to myself was," Oh cool, I get to have a backpack."

When my classmates started obsessing about the test next week, the project next month, the thesis next year; I just stayed in the moment. I bought a day planner instead of month at a glance. I loved the whole process of school and am now counseling—doing the work I was born to do.

When people come to my meetings to lose weight, I tell them to give themselves at least a year to reach their long term goals and start with a few small changes. The person who wants to lose ten pounds might have more abusive food habits than the person with one hundred pounds to lose. It takes the pressure off to have a generous time frame with the focus on just one manageable step at a time.

It's easy to understand why we don't want to take small steps, especially when it comes to weight loss. Small changes take patience. It's hard to be patient if we believe that only the end result has value and the process is torture. We'll go for the quick fix if we think our worth is dependent on our clothing size being a one digit number.

Many of us grew up in families where we were taught that life was a destination where the end result was more important than the journey. Making a habit change or losing a pound at a time seems meaningless in the face of our larger weight loss goal and all the expectations attached to it.

Some of us grew up with chaos and hardship. Life was moment to moment survival without any attention paid to the needs of the future. Setting small goals that lead to calmer peaceful eating practices can seem boring and do not feed the habit of frenzied living that is in our blood.

We can overcome our loyalty to our early programming if we are willing to engage in a process of habit change that takes time. Patience will elude us if we are looking for a magical switch to a willpower button that can instantly transform a lifetime of habits, habits propelled by deep rooted feelings.

Years ago I made a crude version of a Pinocchio puppet that I kept buried in the closet. One day I got it out to show my daughter only to find that the strings were hopelessly tangled. I frantically tried to unravel the mass of knots in one or two maneuvers and failed. My daughter watched in amusement, took the puppet from me and slowly unknotted a string at a time. Her face was aglow with concentration as she relished the challenge. An hour later Pinocchio was free and able to dance in liberation.

Our food obsessions, dysfunctions, and non-pathological habits need patient unraveling. It will take more than an hour but the process itself awakens us to shed our puppet self and become real.

One of my members brought her newborn infant to class. The young mother's eyes were filled with love as she showed us her treasure. As she cradled the baby in her arms, I asked the class to imagine my saying:

Look kid, you have a rough twenty years ahead of you. We're going to expect you to sleep through the night, hold your head up, roll over, sit, stand, walk, talk, give up the breast. It's not going to be easy. Wait 'til those teeth come in. Does that ever hurt! And don't think we're going to dote on you all the time. You'll have a brother or sister to cope with in a couple of years. By then, you better be toilet trained and able to dress yourself. Soon you'll go to nursery school and some of the kids will be mean and tease you. Then comes elementary school. We expect you to be reading fluently and getting good grades. It's never too soon to prepare for college. First you'll have to survive adolescence and deal with zits and hormones. Life isn't a cakewalk, kid, so spit out that pacifier and get real.

If the baby could talk, it would probably say, "No thanks, put me back in the womb."

What we actually do with the newborn is count the tiny fingers and toes and proclaim the little one perfect regardless of the tally. When the baby rolls over, we call the relatives and record it in the baby book. When that kid takes a few wobbly steps and falls we don't scold the baby for clumsiness; we shout and whoop and celebrate this tremendous accomplishment. The first unintelligible words are met with our squeals of delight.

As the baby gets older and life becomes more complicated, it is easy to feel the burden and forget the joy of that budding little being. I can remember when my firstborn would spill sticky apple juice all over the floor. I didn't love wiping it up but I did love him and reminded myself that these precious moments would be over much too soon. When he was toilet training, I viewed the bathroom as the target and his potty chair as the bull's-eye. If he made it to the right room, I cheered.

I was able to focus on the day to day process with my children. It was much harder to do the same for myself. It took time and practice.

When my mom died suddenly eight years ago, I was paralyzed by sorrow. I did what had to be done—went to work, took care of my kids, cooked, went to the grocery store—minimal functioning. What I couldn't do was keep up with the house, mail, errands. I missed routine doctor appointments, soccer registration for my sons, and was late paying bills. The mail piled up and there was clutter everywhere. I would move papers from one area to another but never cleaned up the growing mounds of stuff.

All the clutter was adding to my distress. I remember one morning opening a drawer in the kitchen in search of a pen only to come face to face with a jumble of paper clips, dozens of rubber bands, produce bag twisties from old grocery bags, tangled thread and a hidden tack that pierced my finger. After wiping off the blood and bandaging my wound, I took a few deep breaths and proceeded to tackle the mess.

Out went the dried up marking pens, pencils that were too small to grasp, distorted paper clips, old crayons, a piece of a puzzle that was trashed years ago, zillions of frayed baggie ties, torn newpaper clippings, three dried up marshmallows and a gummy bear covered with fuzz. I even found the missing pen. Naturally, it no longer worked.

I put aside the few items worth saving and dumped everything else into a big trash bag. I felt like a new woman, all cleaned up and ready to deal with my life.

I called my family over to view my great accomplishment. They humored me by pretending to be impressed. No one rolled their eyes or stifled a laugh. The drawer meant nothing to them but they sensed it was really something to me. They saw I was coming back to life.

That little step of cleaning one drawer was a beginning. As I continued to get my house in order, my anxiety slowly decreased, leaving me better able to cope with my grief.

I see life as the "cha-cha." You move a few little steps forward, a few backwards and a few to the side. If you keep on dancing you will notice that by the end of the dance you are not at the place where you started. That's how it goes, forward, backward, side step all across the floor. All those little cha cha cha steps keep you going.

Weight loss is a "cha-cha." You will lose and gain and digress off to the side—a giant side of fries, a fad diet, a binge. If you keep on dancing, you will notice you are at the other side of the room. You've changed some habits, reached some goals, improved your life.

The steps of a baby may be little in distance but they are big in importance, representing major development toward becoming a toddler and eventually a fully grown adult. A baby step doesn't mean something small. It means an important link in a larger chain of development. We can design our own steps of growth in the form of commitments to change that will make a difference in our lives.

For example, research into successful weight loss suggests that keeping a written food record daily is an aid to losing weight. Most of my group members enthusiastically agree with this finding but have major resistance to keeping a food diary no matter what forms and devices we give them to assist the process.

The people who don't ever get into the habit of keeping track of their eating often set themselves up for failure by attempting to do a diary everyday—good intentions but an unrealistic goal that often leads to non-compliance and familiar feelings of despair.

One person in my class decided that once a week would be a good baby step. Her reasoning was in the right direction except the day she picked was Monday, the only day of the week that was never an eating challenge for her. Recording her food on Monday was a bore and gave her no sense of satisfaction.

Another of my students also started with one day. She chose Sunday, her wildest eating day. Writing down everything she ate drastically increased her awareness and curtailed a lot of emotional eating. The baby step wasn't overwhelming but it was enough to give her both challenge and accomplishment. The next week she added Friday night and all of Saturday to cover the weekend. She never did chart the entire week but still was successful in changing her eating habits and losing weight. Perfection is never necessary for progress.

Small developmental change is organic to the young child but takes planning and thought for us as adults. It means being willing to constantly revise goals that are too easy or too hard without wasting our energy on self-flagellation when we don't meet unrealistic attempts at change. It also means correcting our course when it becomes clear that we are trying to meet goals that do not belong to us, and not being thrown off course by over zealous demands of others.

❧

Judy was telling her husband that her weight loss was now a total of forty-eight pounds after fifteen months of step by step progress. Her husband, thinking he was being encouraging, commented, "Just two more pounds and it will be an even fifty."

❧

Rick always felt inferior to his favored older brother who excelled at everything. He gave up attempting to shine in his father's eyes and never felt any pride in his accomplishments as a husband, dad and successful businessman.

Rick played out his longing to be the family star by pushing his only son to go to the prestigious college that his forty-year-old brother attended years ago. He needed the boy to be best in his class, rising above the competition so that years down the road he would qualify for the tough admissions standards of that top school.

The son, who was only ten years old, was filled with tension as he agonized over every homework assignment and panicked at every test. He wanted to make his father proud so he took on his dad's big future goals and could not enjoy the satisfaction of accomplishing the smaller tasks of a young boy. A mistake on the multiplication tables became a disaster for both parent and child.

Fortunately the father sought therapy and began to focus on the issues from the past that drove him to unrealistic expectations. As he recovered from his own childhood hurt, he was able to release his son from an ancient sibling rivalry contest that could have no winners. It took time, but Rick learned to enjoy the pleasures of a loving father-son bond.

Sometimes we attempt unrealistic goals because we hope to fail. We don't really want to do the work involved in making big changes so we set an unattainable goal that will rescue us from our huge demands quickly.

For example, when I wasn't really willing to do what was necessary to eat less in a healthy way, I'd go on a crash diet that would leave me starved and crazed. After a few days, I would "fail" at my efforts to lose weight and give myself permission to feast. I could tell myself that at least I "tried" to lose weight.

When we constantly try and never succeed it means that we are either going after what we don't really want or attempting to get what we want through an impossible process filled with demands and void of encouragement.

I believe we long to treat ourselves like a precious gemstone and celebrate our little victories along the way toward those large goals. Imagine how encouraging it would be if we said to ourselves:

"Good for you. You tried a new vegetable today."

"Give yourself a high five. You got out and took a walk."

"So you gained a couple of pounds. It's okay, it's not the end of the world. "

"Cool! You enrolled in that bungee jumping class you always wanted to take. "

Last winter, I took up skiing after years of letting my fear of the sport keep me off the slopes. I started on the bunny hill with the little kids and stayed at that level until I was ready to move on. I never got to the white knuckle course but did learn to ski well enough to finally join my family in the great frozen outdoors instead of hanging out in the lodge, reading and eating. It was okay with me to go at my pace and become competent not competitive.

One of my group members lost sixty-two pounds and was at her goal weight. She had a very simple formula for success:

The way I finally did it was to keep going and not get crazy when I made a mistake. Just keep going. That's it.

We can put one foot in front of another and just keep going. We can learn to treat ourselves as gently as a newborn. We can applaud each little move in the right direction. We can throw away the dirty diaper but keep the baby.

The product does happen. The child grows to be an adult. The student becomes a teacher. The food addict experiences a peaceful way of eating. Clothing size changes as weight loss becomes weight maintenance. The dream goes from blueprint to substance. We dance as the ballroom of our lives is turning. All it takes is a step at a time.

✪ Be in the Whole
Not the Hole

The guests were gone and we had all kissed goodbye. Alan gave me a high five. The dinner party was a rousing success. I had knocked myself out cooking and was overjoyed with the results.

We were cleaning up while reminiscing about the evening. As I opened the refrigerator to put away leftovers, there was a bag of unused parsley staring up at me. The greens were supposed to be the artistic touch surrounding the chicken. In an eye blink, my good mood shifted and I was filled with despair.

"Alan, you'll never believe what happened. I forgot the parsley."

My unsuspecting husband didn't have a clue regarding the drama of the moment. "So what's the big deal. No one likes parsley anyway."

"It wasn't to eat. It was for decoration. I served the chicken naked."

He rolled his eyes and made an x-rated joke in an attempt to make me feel better. Instead I felt worse—alone in my misery with a husband who obviously didn't get it.

On the surface, what was happening was my creating a fuss over nothing. Obviously, the parsley had no impact on the quality of the evening but internally the situation felt very different. Deep inside I was imagining my friends driving home in the car saying:

It was a nice dinner but it would have been so much better with parsley. That small touch would have told us Dolly cares. I don't know if we should be friends with someone like that. Let's not have anything to do with her ever again."

This absurd scenario was playing deep within the theater of my unconscious. When I saw the parsley and felt anxiety, I didn't know why. The adult rational part of me knew that garnishing the chicken was meaningless but the vulnerable feeling part of me was crushed. I fixated on the hole and could not see the whole. It would be like going into a bagel shop and not seeing any bread, only the empty space at the core of every roll. The substance would be lost.

Another analogy would be imagining looking at a donut and only seeing the hole. But when it comes to donuts, the distortion is often the opposite. We see the pastry part and ignore the emptiness at the center. We want to believe that consuming one of those puffy sugary blobs can fill our holes only to find ourselves unfulfilled, wanting more and eating to the point of indigestion without any relief.

The sight of the parsley activated my inside holes. My old behavior would have been to eat, consuming the leftovers instead of putting them away. This time I faced those old demons that filled me with shame, determined to stay strong.

Gradually my anxiety lifted and my perspective changed. I took a good look at my husband and saw his efforts to cheer me up as helpful not hurtful. It didn't take long to retrieve my initial good feelings about the evening. I was even able to put away the leftovers without becoming a human garbage dump.

The next morning I woke up feeling at peace instead of in pieces. Later that day I chopped up the errant parsley and tossed it with diced tomatoes, onions, lemon and olive oil. It made a great salad.

It's easy for me to accept others in good times and bad. My clients and students tell me how safe they feel in my presence because they know I would never put them down for their mistakes. Yet it took me years before I could embrace my own "holiness."

The sight of the parsley triggered what I call an "Alice In Wonderland" experience. We fall down an emotional hole and land in a crazy world with no visible way out. Just like Alice we begin to shrink and lose our way. Whenever there is a jolt of strong emotion that the mind knows is irrational it is often a sign that something going on in the present has sucked us back into the past.

A friend wanted to treat me to a birthday lunch at her country club. We walked in together and everyone acknowledged her as she confidently led the way to our seats. I lagged behind and started to feel uneasy as I looked around. At one table I could see golfers with their polo shirts and designer slacks. At another table were the tennis players with their matching shorts and tops. Everyone began to look alike and I felt totally out of place. Anyone glancing my way would instantly know I was neither an athlete nor a member of any country club.

When the waiter asked for my order, I could barely answer. My usually strong voice was a whisper as I requested the same thing as my friend. This was not typical behavior for me and I knew I had to get a grip. So I excused myself and retreated to the safety of the restroom.

I sprinkled cold water on my face and asked myself a question that always leads into the heart of what is going on when my behavior doesn't make sense: "Is it real or is it Memorex?" Almost instantly, I was traveling back on an emotional bridge across the years to the time when I felt the same way as I was feeling now.

The memories that came to me were from elementary school when I was an outsider longing to fit in. My parents had come to Los Angeles from Greece bringing their old world ways. They spoke broken English and struggled to survive after losing so much in the Holocaust.

Money was scarce so my mother made all my clothes using whatever fabric was cheapest. She had reams of this unfashionable orange material that became the base for most of my outfits. My Brownie uniform wasn't a uniform. It was a pair of handmade brown shorts and a T-shirt because that was what we could afford. In those days, all I wanted was to look like everyone else.

The country club took me right into the wound of those years when I felt like an outsider. Once the memory was retrieved, I could release it and remind myself that I wasn't six anymore. Then I could accept my role as an invited guest about to have lunch in a beautiful setting.

I went back to the table with my grown-up eyes and took another look around. There were no tennis or golf uniforms and the members were not caricatures of the pampered rich. As I began to listen to the conversation, I realized that many of the people at my table were just like me—hard workers who had a rare few hours free. As we laughed together, I understood that belonging had nothing to do with having a membership card.

The question, "Is it real or is it Memorex?" is a way to bring ourselves out of the past so we can open our eyes to the reality of the present. Having a way to remind ourselves that we have fallen down the hole of yesterday gives us a chance to soothe our younger self, brush off the dirt and climb back into the whole of today.

I was in a tiny toy shop about to exit through the narrow aisle leading to the door. A young woman was standing in the middle of the aisle blocking the pathway out. I politely said, "Excuse me" as I started to go around her to leave the store.

The woman stuck her hands on her hips and stared at me in defiance. "No," she said, "I'm not moving." She stood with her feet apart and made it impossible for me to pass.

I was speechless. In a zillion crowded aisle encounters, I had never come across such rudeness. I tried humor and charm but she stared me down and remained firmly entrenched. I gave up and found another way out by going around the back of the cash register in an area not intended for customers. I felt humiliated and shaken way beyond what I would expect from such a small incident. I knew it was a memorex moment but couldn't quite figure out why.

My feelings seemed old and primitive. It was as though this stranger was a bully from another time when we were kids together in a room full of toys that she wanted all to herself. I was afraid she would beat me up if I came into her space.

When I walked out of the store, I was standing in the middle of a block loaded with kiddie food—an ice cream parlour, candy shop, donut store, hot dog stand--all the comfort foods that would ease my anxiety. I wanted everything but knew that I would only end up feeling worse by using junk food as a tranquilizer. So I went to my car and sat there motionless as the feelings moved through me, bringing tears.

As the time lengthened, my desire to eat faded along with the intensity of my feelings. I opened my purse, took out my driver's license and looked at my picture and birthdate to remind myself that I was now an adult strong enough to handle the little slights of everyday living.

Using perspective to soothe our feelings is a powerful way to keep us from getting stuck in old holes from the past. We can also transform the pull of the past by reframing stressful situations. A new frame on an old picture can totally change our reaction to the content of the picture.

One of my members totally transformed what could have been a constant source of misery by reframing her experience. She was transferred by her company from a suburb near her home to downtown Los Angeles, a drive of about ninety minutes through heavy traffic.

The long commute took her right back to unpleasant memories from her childhood when her family would travel two hours back and forth to visit her grandmother. She loved her grandma but hated the ride. Her parents wouldn't let her eat in the car or play games and there was never a bathroom stop. She would often get car sick. The ride to work brought back all those old feelings.

She wanted to create a positive experience of commuting to compete with the old memories. One of the best aspects of her new location was that her co-workers were from many different cultures. She was very excited about the diversity of her new work place.

She decided to pretend that she was traveling to a different country each morning. One day she imagined she was going to India because there were people she worked with from India. The next day it would be Mexico or Italy, Thailand or Greece. There were over twenty countries represented in her office. She would play available audio tapes that featured music from some of the countries and began to learn Spanish on tape as she drove to work because there were many Hispanic people living in the neighborhood where the office was located.

She told her co-workers what she was doing and about her interest in their cultures. Before long, she and her new colleagues had organized weekly pot luck lunches featuring food from different countries. Her emotional reaction to the long car ride soon went from anxiety to anticipation.

This member of my class was also in the process of getting rid of over fifty excess pounds. She was determined to make her new work situation pleasant so that she would not arrive home from work every evening in a vulnerable, hungry, little-kid state of mind.

By taking a positive perspective, she did not deny the reality of the long commute but sought an aspect of her situation that could fill her emotionally instead of turning to food for that purpose.

One of the biggest holes we fall into is believing in an idealized version of ourselves as perfect—a superior being who could never forget the parsley garnish. In my off again on again diet days, I would fantasize every weekend about how pure my eating would be starting Monday with the weight just dropping off like falling leaves.

I would fall asleep Sunday night calculating my spectacular weight loss. By morning I had lost thirty pounds in fantasy and felt total commitment toward being the ideal dieter. My breakfast was a high fiber low calorie cereal with nonfat milk and half a grapefruit. Virtue was oozing out of every pore.

Then the day would go on and I'd have a little taste of this and a bite of that and soon the negative tirade inside my head would start: "You blew it. Now you can't have fish for dinner. You might as well have pizza with the kids."

It took me many years to get out that kind of hole and learn a more positive way to deal with myself without setting up unrealistically high expectations that always brought me low. One of the lighter ways I get myself out of the perfect dieter hole is by confessing my crazy ways.

The other night my husband Alan and I went to the movies. As he headed to the refreshment stand, I looked at him and smugly announced my intention to eat nothing but sips of bottled water. Five minutes into the previews, I was flipping out from inhaling popcorn fumes and excused myself to go to the restroom. On the way back, I bought a little box of chocolate covered raisins because they would be quiet to eat. I took them out of the box and stuck them on top of a kleenex in my purse. Whenever there would be laughter in the movie, I'd go, "Ha, ha," and throw some raisins in my mouth. Alan never caught on nor did he care because he was busy with his popcorn.

As we drove home, I told him about the raisins and we had a good laugh. I wasn't a sinner and didn't want my attempt at snackless movie viewing to result in deception. Confession was much more fun.

In *Webster's Dictionary,* the first definition of the word hole is "an opening through something." As we create new perspectives we can go through our holes into the healing space of wholeness.

⌛ The Waiting Game

The phone jolted me awake. It was Katie's voice. "Mom, it's me. I'm coming back today. Aren't you excited?"

"Honey, it's five in the morning. I'll do excitement when the sun comes up."

"Oh Mom, I forgot about the time difference. I can't wait to come home."

Katie was returning from a school trip to Washington D.C. and would arrive mid afternoon. Alan and I would leave for the airport in a few hours. I was in an upbeat mood, looking forward to having our youngest safely back in the nest.

The time passed easily as I was busy with my usual Saturday routine. Then Katie called again to say she was stuck in the airport because the plane was delayed due to bad weather. She wasn't sure when she would arrive in L.A.

Now I started "waiting," carrying the phone around with me, checking with the airline every half hour, worrying. I was thrown back to my childhood when my mother would panic any time my father was a few minutes late.

"Where's daddy? Where's daddy? Something must have happened to daddy." She would wring her hands and pace the floor, checking the window anytime a car passed. As an adult, I understand that her behavior was typical of a holocaust survivor; but as a kid, I just got caught up in the fear with her.

I felt that old panic about Katie. Maybe we shouldn't have let her go. Visions of my daughter on a plane streaking through blinding snowstorms filled me with terror. Alan had taken our sons out for lunch so I could have peace and quiet. Now I felt isolated and panicky.

In the past, I would have handled my anxiety by eating. The eating would be an activity to deal with "the waiting place," that scary space between the cracks of life.

Before I lost fifty pounds, it would have been chips, cookies, candy—all the foods that make little kids happy. When I was losing weight, I switched to plain popcorn, rice cakes and baby carrots. The food change was healthier but the behavior was the same. I couldn't stand the void of waiting. It touched my own empty places and I didn't know how to cope.

My experience with Katie and the plane is typical of "disaster preparedness" waiting. We have some anxiety about an impending event and create worst case scenarios. We are filled with visions of doom. Eating soothes the immediate stress but does nothing to ease the deeper concerns.

As we wait in the stillness, old primitive feelings of sadness and isolation wash over us in waves of pain. We are waiting for the sorrow to ease, for the loneliness to cease, for the disaster to end happily.

Much of our waiting is not disaster-related. We get thrown by that ordinary experience of empty time we call "boredom". We're waiting for something routine and don't know how to fill the space. The moments are without drama or trauma.

We've eaten breakfast and long for the next meal, snacking to ease the angst. We sit at the movie theater restlessly wanting the movie to begin, eating handfuls of popcorn before the coming attractions even hit the screen. We arrive early for an appointment and find ourselves restlessly wandering to the vending machine to get a little something.

As long as there is the next bite, we are engrossed and don't have to struggle to find better ways to spend the nickle and dime moments of life.

It's difficult for me to be waiting because waiting means nothing is happening. If nothing is happening, then I'm not happening. I'm waiting to feel better, different, acceptable. I don't understand that the waiting—in my own skin, in my own stillness, is what is supposed to be happening. It is the emotional task of the moment.

It's as if I'm a trapeze artist way up in space alone. I've let go of one swing and am flying through endless nothingness toward the next swing. I'm in mid air unable to feel me, unaware of anything else but the void. I can't feel my worth. I don't exist in that moment in between swings. Waiting is timeless, devoid of structure and often terrifying.

In the real circus, the audience is also waiting as the trapeze artist is flying from one swing to another. That few seconds between can seem endless to the spectators who gasp and momentarily stop breathing as the anticipation mounts.

Usually there is a safety net that could offer comfort from the innate fear of death that the trapeze artist triggers in that moment of letting go of the bar. Sometimes there is no safety net or it is forgotten as attention is focused high in the air where the drama is unfolding. The safety net is there but below the point of awareness. The sense of danger is felt in the midst of safety.

In our lives, the waiting places bring up penetrating questions. Notice your gut level response as you ask yourself: Am I up too high or not high enough? Am I swinging too fast or going too slow? Is there a safety net? Did I let go too soon or is the time to let go over? Will I survive? Will I touch the lives of the audience? Will my life be worth applauding?"

Our most tragic waiting occurs when we put off our healthy yearnings until we are satisfied with our weight. I'll never forget Dana, a member of one of my groups. One session she burst into tears and told of a twenty year wish that was never fulfilled because she was waiting to be thin. It was easy to relate to her story:

> I always wanted one of those formal portraits of the whole family with everyone dressed to the nines and the kids in matching velvet outfits. I made dozens of appointments with the photographer that were cancelled at the last moment because I was still fat and didn't want to ruin the picture. The kids are grown up now and it's too late.

"Dana," I said, "It's too late for yesterday's picture but it is never too late. Grab those grownup kids and put them in velvet outfits right now. Then march over to the mall and have the picture taken. You've waited long enough."

Dana refused to give us any follow-up for weeks. Then one evening she walked into the meeting room carrying a large package wrapped in brown paper. She tore off the wrapping to reveal a magnificent portrait, everyone dressed in the finest of formal attire including her baby grand-daughter who had on a red velvet gown. Dana looked like a queen sitting in the center of her stunning family. She felt regret over waiting so long but had to admit that later was better than never.

Sometimes we must wait because we were not in charge of granting our wishes. When I was young, there was no use in my wanting the cool clothes or possessions my friends had. My parents taught me to make do with homemade everything and be grateful for the roof over my head and the food on the table. Most of the time I could stifle my childish wants but not when it came to the fad item that captured my heart—Mary Jane shoes.

I fell madly in love with those shiny patent leather shoes with the ankle strap that every girl in my elementary school class seemed to own but me. I had cute little feet and could just imagine myself dancing around the room like a princess. I just had to have them.

As always, my parents considered my wanting frivolous and selfish. The answer was no even when I came up with ways to earn the money myself. My parents came from a world of hardship where they couldn't understand how some wants of the heart were just as important as physical necessities.

The years went by and the shoes were forgotten until about a year ago. I was in a mall and there they were—the same Mary Jane shoes that I craved all those years ago. My feet were much older but still small and cute. My waiting was over as I bought those shoes that meant so much to me when I was ten. I left the mall feeling so full that I didn't even walk by the food park on the way out.

I've never worn those shoes because they no longer fit my taste or need for comfort but it gives me great pleasure just to know they are safe in my closet where I can look at them and remember that little girl who still yearns to be cherished and understood.

❧

Many of us engage in "anticipatory waiting" based on good intentions for self-improvement that initially motivate a flurry of activity but eventually overwhelm us. We have a long list with many weight-related items on it along with other changes that we believe will get us closer to our ideal self.

On that list are items that may seem very worthwhile, such as starting a healthy eating program, joining a gym, getting a degree, finding a better job, expanding our social circle, redecorating, doing volunteer work, doing, doing, doing, doing. The list can be as endless and frustrating as New Year resolutions that stay buried in a drawer where we can't see them but know they exist. They become clutter for the soul.

Sometimes we are eating to delay entering the process of positive change while our guilt increases as time passes. The food is easy to obtain filling us up for the moment so that the emptiness of unfulfilled desires doesn't hurt so much.

Some of our dreams are healthy and all we need is to take that first step that moves us from procrastination to process. Other items on that long self-improvement list come from our waiting to be anyone but who we are. We are wanting to be different and never feel as if we are enough right now. No matter how high we climb, we always see another mountain to be conquered before we can rest and enjoy the rich solid ground we are standing on.

We are waiting to feel better, good enough to be in our own skins, in our own stillness without wanting to escape. How painful it is when we say to ourselves: "Tomorrow I will be different. I will be someone else, someone better, thinner, richer, smarter and more productive. Tomorrow I will be loved. Tomorrow I will be enough."

Our work is to embrace ourselves today and stop the waiting games that rob us of time and energy. If we can wait without an agenda, we can find our quiet--our way of growing that is healthy not toxic.

Imagine being able to say to yourself:

Today you are good enough just as you are. Your looks are enough. Your efforts are just right. You spread love in this world. If everyone were like you, we wouldn't have crime or wars or world hunger. There would be no child abuse or discrimination or cruelty. You are a treasure of a human being and I appreciate you just as you are. You make the world a better place for everyone.

We are afraid that if we give up waiting to be better, we'll stop growing and doing anything positive. When we stop eating over the pain of rejecting who we are today and embrace ourselves, we can regain the biological knowing we had as an infant that growth is what human beings are born to do.

❧

Not all waiting games are unhealthy. It helps to use our creativity to convince ourselves to wait when we are gravitating toward old habits of emotional eating.

The other day I was at the mall very goal-directed in my search for a birthday gift for a friend. I came out of a large department store, mission accomplished, and was heading for the exit when my senses were assaulted by an unexpected image.

A sparkling new pretzel shop had just opened up in the corridor leading to the exit. A grandmotherly looking woman was smiling as she handed out large pieces of that hot buttery delicacy to the group of shoppers gathered around her. Everyone looked pleased—part of something wonderful. I looked at this happy communal scene from the distance and felt an old yearning. It was bread and butter and love calling to my hungriest youngest self. It was being connected to the group, not being left out. It was also time for a waiting game.

So I had a chat with that part of me that was willing to sell my soul for a bite of bread:

Dolly, you can have the pretzel if you really want it, but let's wait awhile. Take the package to the car and put it away. Go for a walk around the block and feel the sunshine. Then if you still want the pretzel, go back in, have it and enjoy it.

As soon as I walked out of the mall, the pretzel image lost its power. I saw my car and remembered the errands left to run and the healthy lunch waiting for me at home. Even if I had chosen to go back and take a sample of pretzel, it would have been out of choice not compulsion.

Finding ways to wait out my emotional urges to eat is a game that I don't always win, but each small victory makes the next challenge easier.

Let's go back now to that tiny moment of waiting a few years ago when Katie's plane was flying through stormy weather. She did arrive home safely and we had a joyous reunion. I managed to survive the wait without turning to food. It wasn't easy. I felt that old primal anxiety and had to remind myself to exhale. I tried to stop worrying but couldn't turn off the "Where's Daddy?" tapes from my childhood.

After struggling awhile, I walked across the street and stayed with a neighbor who is as nurturing as chicken soup. She was able to listen and sit with me as I worried and waited in my own separate skin. Her loving presence did not take away my anxiety but she did provide much more comfort than the emptiness of a feeding frenzy. Soon Alan and the boys came home and we were on the way to the airport to pick up Katie.

Waiting is not a game. If we choose to kill time with food, we are also killing off the opportunity that waiting gives us. It can be a time for reflection and life-affirming choices. The moments between spaces are times to build bridges across the gaps so we can feel safe and whole.

Scale Madness Weighs Heavy On the Heart

"Mirror, mirror on the wall, who is the fairest of them all. . ."

To the constant dieter, it is the scale more than the mirror that reflects our image back to us. We long to hear:

You, you are the fairest of them all. You are perfect in every way.

The majority of people who come to my meetings allow themselves to be weighed before the lecture begins. The weigh-in is not absolutely mandatory but for people attempting to lose weight, scale encounters become part of a ritual enacted weekly, daily or endlessly. It is at the scale that the deepest dramas of our lives play out.

The scale is just a fallible piece of machinery that tells us our weight at the moment. It is not a measure of character or behavior. It doesn't care what we ate or how we ate it. It doesn't adjust to the glass of water consumed before weighing or recognize pre-menstrual bloat. A pounds off coupon is never given to account for those exercise 'till you drop muscles that weigh heavier than fat. That skinny scale has no heart, no soul and no interest in our stories of virtue or vice. Yet we give it Godlike power over our lives.

It is sad that we allow the number on the scale to determine our self-worth as though it is a measure of who we are—the bigger the number, the smaller our value as a person. We allow something very insignificant to tell us if we are significant.

The scale is like a grade on a test. It triggers off deep feelings from the past about being judged and coming up short in comparison to others. For many of us, the number on the scale will impact our mood for moments, hours or even days. The scale takes on human proportions, becoming a source of reward or punishment. Our lives are on the line as we hold our breath and prepare to receive our fate.

I can remember attending this scrumptious banquet with my husband at a time when I was into being the "perfect" dieter. I had the Caesar salad without the dressing, passed up the steaming onion rolls, took the crust off the Chicken Wellington and didn't even inhale the hot fudge brownie creation that was dessert. I felt ready for sainthood and leapt on the scale as soon as we got home. I don't know what I expected--that confetti would pop out as my monumental weight loss was revealed.

I still can feel the shock of looking down at the number and seeing a gain of one pound. At that moment, I was just a hurt little kid crying out, "It's not fair. It's just not fair."

The scale pushes lots of buttons. We get very upset if it isn't a caring mommy bearing a reward of weight loss when we are good. After major overeating, we approach the scale with fear while holding onto the hope that there will be no punishment; we will be rewarded anyway. If there is weight loss when we expect a gain, that often pushes us to get cocky and overeat more, testing to see what we can get away with before getting busted.

The scale also pushes our "entitlement" buttons. When we follow a weight loss program, we not only expect to lose weight but want the pounds off to be substantial. Typical scale talk sounds like this:

"What, I only lost one pound, I was so good this week."

"Two pounds, last week it was three. I'm doing something wrong."

"Half a pound, what's the point of even trying."

"I gained. That can't be. I was so perfect."

When we work so hard—drink the eight glasses of water, order the salad dressing on the side, say no to a greasy hamburger or a fabulous dessert, refuse to give in to impulsive food desires; we believe that we are now owed a weight loss. The world must reward us for our sacrifices.

This sense of entitlement that presses our fairness buttons cuts across areas of living that go beyond the scale. It was quite a revelation to me to see how my own sense of entitlement spilled over into the work place.

My office is in a building that uses parking attendants. I use one hour validation stickers for those times when I'm in and out rather than parked for the whole day.

I've developed a friendly relationship with the young guys that park the car. I always acknowledge them, make eye contact, joke around, offer them gum and other treats. I don't just dump my car in an impersonal way. The guys seem to like me and I get lots of high fives as I come and go.

One day I came down to the lot and handed my validation card to one of the young attendants who was chomping on the gum I had given him. He waved hello and then let me know that I needed another sticker to cover the minutes past the one hour.

"You must be kidding," I said laughingly, "It was only an extra six minutes. Can't you cut me some slack?" I felt so sure that I would be given extra special treatment because I was such a beloved customer. It would have been nice but the entitlement code was only in my mind not the reality of the situation.

I wanted to scream, "Don't you remember who I am? I'm the one who gives you gum and licorice, the one with the jokes and the friendly smile. You owe me. I'm so nice, so good."

I paid the extra hour sticker and continued to behave in a friendly way because no one wronged me. My need for the world to revolve around my vision of justice was my issue, not that of the parking attendant who was just doing his job as instructed. It was healthy for me to be reminded that my good behavior doesn't automatically entitle me to have my way.

No matter how many years we have spent overweight, we have a deep belief that when we make even minor changes, the results should be instantaneous and huge. In our little kid heart, we want to wake up the next morning thin. Underneath our wanting is the wish for unconditional love even though that only happens to people who own dogs.

When we are at the scale, it is as though our lives are on the line. The scale becomes the good or bad parent who will tell us if we are worthy of love. We are waiting to hear if they are proud of us. When we have been good and have "given up so much" we are devastated if we are punished by receiving a number that feels like an F on the exam of life. When we believe we deserve a reward and do not get it, there is that sense that all our hard work was for nothing and our goodness has been met with betrayal.

When we approach the scale knowing that our eating was over the top and that a weight gain is inevitable, there is still that primal longing for a good parent who will overlook our behavior and love us anyway. We expect a cold inanimate object that measures our pounds to have a heart and soul even though we know better.

In my on-again-off-again dieting days, I used to weigh myself all the time. I would get up in the morning and head right for the scale, letting the tally determine if it was going to be a day of feast or famine. My sense of well being would be totally influenced by the number. I would jiggle around and move the location of the scale trying to maneuver the verdict in my favor.

In the early days of being a member of Weight Watchers, I would wear flimsy lightweight clothes in preparation for the weekly scale encounter. Off would go my earrings, watch and wedding ring as I did a semi-striptease before stepping on the platform and facing the number. I was playing no-win games to ward off my anxiety.

Some of my friends have never had weight problems and don't even own a scale. If their clothes feel tight, they automatically cut back on their eating or else make peace with wearing a larger size. They don't give their power to an object.

Many members of my classes talk about months or years when they never stepped on a scale because they didn't want to face the harsh reality of a number that would verify what they already knew about their size. Many of them also avoided getting medical exams because of panic over having to be weighed.

I got rid of my home scale during the time I was attending Weight Watchers. It was the only way to stop my behavior of scale hopping a zillion times a day. Life was easier when I only confronted the scale during a weekly weigh-in at a meeting and had no means to compulsively check myself at home.

There were times I would attend a meeting but not get weighed because I felt too vulnerable to face the scale. Usually, I could confront the consequences of my eating behavior but needed the freedom to skip the scale during those ultra-sensitive times. However, I always forced myself to go to a meeting for support, no matter how intense my desire to stay home might be.

My old style had been to avoid going to a meeting if my eating had been less than perfect. It was similar to my needing to clean the house just before the cleaning crew was coming. I had to cut through my layers of guilt and shame to be able to reach out for help. We need to do whatever it takes so that we don't let our fear of the scale keep us from the places of support where we can thrive.

Here's what I tell my class members about weighing:

I want you to use the "whatever" method of handling the scale. Remember it is fickle and not always reflective of what you have done in the short term. So if it is up, say, "whatever." If it stays the same, "whatever." If the pounds go down, don't get so excited. What goes down can come back up. That's a whatever moment, too. Let "whatever" be your mantra as you weigh in without the drum roll and violins.

As for constant weighing on your home scale, glue a piece of paper with your ideal weight over the window where the numbers appear. Each time you scale hop, say to yourself. "Great, I'm right where I want to be. Now let me go out and do my life."

Then I add:

If you think you have gained weight, don't avoid coming to our meeting where we can help you help yourself. You don't have to lose weight to be worthy of support. The scale won't give you love, but we will at the meeting if you will fight the forces of shame that make you want to hide. Just keep showing up.

The scale does give valid information over several weeks about weight only, nothing else. Pounds off over time are an opportunity to reflect on behaviors worth continuing. Weight gaining and plateaus are not about lack of character but about the need to problem solve and make some changes.

I can remember when one of my sons got a below average grade on a test and was very upset. "Mom, I just don't get it. I can't believe I got this grade."

I didn't say to him, "What's wrong with you? Why didn't you study harder? Let's ground you." I did tell him I was sorry he was hurting and then we looked together at what might have happened and what could be done in the future. He came up with a strategy to improve the next test score. Getting a better grade on the next test felt good to my son but so did the process of problem solving in a positive way without resorting to personal put downs.

It is human to feel disappointment when the scale reflects slow or no weight loss. The immediate reaction is not the problem. It is when we don't use our inner resources to move beyond the initial reaction that gets us into extreme behavior such as bingeing, quitting a healthy eating plan, avoiding social engagements and many other ways we have to act out against our best interests.

One of my members said:

I try to think of the scale as irrelevant. I know when I'm bloated or my clothes are getting tight. I know when I'm into crazy eating. I want to get rid of the bad habits and feel good in my body. So I am totally into the "whatever" method regarding the number on the scale. If I feel bad about my behavior, weight loss doesn't make me feel good. If I feel good about my behavior, a weight gain doesn't burst my bubble.

A determined member in one of my groups reached her weight goal of a ten pound weight loss. She got up and put it all into perspective for us:

I've tried to lose this weight quickly by crazy dieting and always failed. It took me a year to lose only ten pounds but in that year my whole life changed. I learned how to take my little girl to the beach and go swimming with her instead of hiding under a towel. I've experienced the pleasure of eating healthy, clean, tasty food. I'm out there power walking four times a week and pump iron like a jock. I'm in a good mood around my husband instead of being the witch from diet hell. I look in the mirror and see my essence not just a bunch of fat cells. I've become the person I always wanted to be. It's just ten pounds but it feels like I've released the weight of the world off my shoulders.

When we look inside to find our goodness, then we can feel worthy regardless of the length of time it takes to solve complex eating issues. We can learn to stop equating our progress as a human being to the weight of our flesh or size of our jeans.

"Scale, scale on the floor . . ."

We are weighing the momentary pull of the gravity we exert on the earth, not our impact on the world. When I weigh myself, I like to imagine a nurturing motherly voice saying to me:

Honey, let's celebrate the number. After all, you're worth your weight in gold!

Waste of Food
Or Waste of Life

Separating from food is one thing. Killing it is another. "Thou shalt not murder." I knew that commandment well.

A few years ago my daughter Katie had her *Bat Mitzvah.* Our family was left with many mementos, among them a large slab of cake topped with frosting words of congratulations. I carefully wrapped this precious leftover and placed it in the freezer for safe keeping. Frozen cake tastes delicious so I found myself slithering and shaving the slab each time I came in the kitchen. Something had to be done. I tried to pawn it off on my husband and kids.

"Who wants cake? How about you Alan?"

"Have a slice, Robby. You're a growing boy."

"Aron, let's pack some up for your trip back to college."

"Katie, it's your special cake. Enjoy."

No takers. I was the only one interested. Alan came to my rescue by offering to take it with him to the office in the morning. Of course, he forgot. It was now Monday after the big weekend and I was feeling the let down. The cake was calling to me, screaming my name.

I paged my husband and became a wild woman on the phone:

Alan, how could you do this to me? You drove off without the cake. You promised you'd take it with you. I can't believe you could forget something so important. Is this what you call love?

My long-suffering mate tried to defend himself but had no clue as to what he had done. He offered to put the cake in the car as soon as he got home. I knew it would be too late. I took the cake and threw it down the garbage disposal. I watched "Katie" dissolve as the running water swept away my daughter's frosting name. I heard grinders pulverizing the hard hunk of cake without mercy.

I felt like a murderer and it wasn't until much later that my guilt was replaced by an uneasy sense of peace. I knew deep inside that I was better off dumping the cake than wearing it.

I told the members of my classes the story. I expected them to understand the part about guilt over wasted food because many of them had grown up as members of the "Clean Your Plate, Save the Starving Children Club." What shocked me was how many people identified with my irrational feeling that the cake was a living being that had been killed off. The comments were mind boggling:

"When I save food from a special occasion, it is preserving a memory. When I eat it later, the memory becomes part of my tissues. Throwing it away is losing a cherished piece of my life."

"I adore cookies and chocolate. Each cookie is a friend. Chocolate is more like a lover. If I throw any of them away, I feel as though I have discarded a person."

"I can toss out some foods but not others. I have no problem with old vegetables or smelly fish. I can discard egg whites but not the yolks. The yolks are the substance. I can't snuff out the life force of the egg."

"If I throw away a food I want, it is as though it is gone from the planet. I have killed off a member of an endangered species."

I told my cake story to ten classes made of people from a variety of ethnic and socioeconomic groups and the responses were remarkably similar. No wonder guilt was running so deep if food disposal feels like murder.

Consuming more than we need isn't limited to food. It took me both time and therapy to be able to throw away anything at all. My father was a concentration camp survivor and my mother was in hiding during the time of the Holocaust. A scrap of bread could mean the difference between life and death.

My mom was a recycler before it became popular. Stale milk became a cake ingredient, orange peels turned into jam, leftovers were transformed into casseroles. Worn out torn clothing became rags. Old newspapers were piled high awaiting future use. Nothing was wasted. This was my childhood and I learned the lessons well.

This anxiety over any type of waste was very evident when my mother would come over to visit the grandchildren. I'd be cleaning up from their lunch and she'd be grabbing gooey toast crusts or spitty mashed potato bits from the dirty dishes. "Mom. You don't need to eat that. Sit down, let me make you a fresh plate."

She would take the fresh plate only after consuming the crumbs. She could not be witness to the discarding of "perfectly good food." My mother was very heavy and died of a heart attack in her early seventies, much too soon for those of us who loved her.

I don't have to save everything anymore. It has become easy for me to give away clothes and possessions because they can be donated to a charity. Old newspapers and magazines can go to a recycle station. That doesn't feel like waste. But I still struggle with some items and in that struggle confront the same issues that surround my excesses with food.

It is almost impossible for me to part with anything that has a message meant for me. My closets are bulging with boxes of greeting cards. Those simple words: "Thinking of you," "Happy Birthday," "To My Sweetheart," "Happy Mother's Day," "Wish You Were Here,"—are tangible evidence that I matter. It feels like throwing out love to discard any of my paper treasures. In my unconscious there must be an image of myself as a very old woman in my rocking chair, totally alone in the world, going over every one of those cards to remind myself that once I was someone who was loved.

Underneath the unhealthy holding on that afflicts so many of us lies the false belief that there is a scarcity of our vital supplies, especially food and love. Food keeps us alive physically and love makes life worth living. Our deepest unspoken fear is that our resources will be used up and we will be left isolated, unwanted and starving.

I also can't throw out photos, not even the blurry underdeveloped pictures that are barely recognizable. To throw away pictures of my family and friends is like throwing them away. The greeting cards represent love coming to me while the photographs symbolize my love flowing for others.

Throwing away the image of someone I care about feels like I'm tossing away the relationship. The pictures connect me to the people and places in the images. In order to throw away a picture, I need to feel secure in my ability to hold loved ones inside so that I won't need endless tangible reminders that we are connected.

Many people in my classes could relate to the universal issue of tension between holding on and letting go. My example of the photos generated lots of head nodding and comments. One woman sadly related her experience:

> I can't throw away pictures either unless I'm in them. I'm great at throwing away photos of myself. When I was cleaning the attic, I found boxes of old pictures--priceless momentos except for those that were evidence of my years as a fat kid. I tore up all the pictures of that long ago little girl. Now I'm sorry because my kids hungrily devour those family pictures and want to know why there are so few of me. I threw away a part of their history along with my own.

It is easy for us to be confused about what to save and what to discard. We think throwing away half of box of stale cookies is wasteful but never thought purchasing it was a waste of money. Buying boxes of girl scout cookies or chocolate bars at a school drive feels like our civic duty even though it will cost us a big chunk of emotional energy as we struggle to not devour the whole thing. We know these organizations will accept donations without our taking the products but that option seems unthinkable.

❧

One of my members tried an experiment for a month. She would go grocery shopping as usual but when she arrived at the checkout stand, she removed all food from her cart that was purchased impulsively for emotional eating. She included all junk food in this category. She tallied the amount of money saved and purchased donation coupons equal to that amount. These are pledge coupons available at the checkout stand right next to the candy bars and gossip magazines. The money amount on the coupon is donated to an organization that feeds the homeless. At the end of the month, she had donated over thirty dollars and lost eight pounds.

Separating from food gets easier with practice. A way to begin is just by paying attention to what is happening in your eating life.

Notice your behavior: What are you buying? What are you actually consuming? Are you ever able to throw away unwanted or unhealthy food without emotional upheaval? What is different about the times you are in harmony with food, taking in and letting go without feeling deprived or driven to excess?

We are so used to noticing what we are doing that is undesirable that we don't take the time to understand the strengths we already possess. It is easy to believe we have no skills when we feel bad about our eating or weight but noticing our behavior usually reveals many good habits.

Sometimes practicing imaginary situations helps us with the real thing. I like rehearsing in my head. One of my practice scenarios is to imagine I'm out to dinner with a friend. I'm full but there is still food left on my plate. I can't take anything home because I'm going to the North Pole for a month and the refrigerator will be turned off.

I beg my friend to eat the leftovers but she is not interested. She also refuses my suggestion that she take a doggy bag home. I ultimately must ask the waiter to take my plate away. I have chosen to separate from the remaining food and not make it part of my body. There is space between me and the leftovers. I watch with longing as the food disappears from view when the waiter walks away toward the kitchen. I grieve the loss for a few seconds and then it is over.

Try out the following imaginary but very realistic scenario to test your own reactions to throwing out food:

Imagine that you arrive at a meeting after eating a satisfying meal. A plate filled with huge chocolate chip cookies is passed around.

You're not hungry but they look great so you take one. After a few bites, you've had enough and involve yourself fully in the meeting. Just as the meeting is winding down, the trash basket is passed. You want to dump the cookie but have feelings about throwing it away.

Feel the feelings as you toss it in the trash and see it crumbling there dirty and discarded. Notice your reaction as the trash is being removed from sight. See yourself surviving just fine, going on with your life free from any thoughts of the cookie.

Another version of the same scenario would be to imagine yourself not taking the cookie at all. You are full from a meal that included dessert and don't really want a sugary snack less than an hour later. Picture yourself "throwing away" an opportunity to take the free dessert. Notice your reaction to seeing other people eating cookies as you stick with your choice not to have one. (If cookies don't excite you, substitute another treat in your fantasy.)

The cookie situation may seem simple but it is those little morsel moments that occur throughout the day that can constantly lead us into choices that go against what we really want for health and well being.

Our attachments to food go back to our earliest memories. Did we get enough? Did our parents or caretakers beam when we ate all the food they put before us? Were they angry if we pushed the plate away? Was it subtle—a look of disappointment when we didn't want a second helping of homemade pie or failed to show enthusiasm for the tuna casserole?

Some of us were punished or shamed if we didn't eat everything put on our plates. We learned that the empty plate would fill us with love not just food. If we didn't eat the food that our mommies and daddies gave us, they might throw us away. When we were babies they controlled our feedings and taking back that control means separating from those grown ups who were once our link to survival.

Some of us clean the plate because we never got enough. There were too many mouths to feed or we were punished by being sent to bed without supper. Perhaps we were taunted about our size and told not to eat so much. We don't trust that there will be enough to fill us. We consume everything now because we don't know what tomorrow will bring. Maybe the candy store will burn down. Maybe the chef will quit and run away with the recipe. Maybe tomorrow won't come.

Sometimes life with food seems like an "all you can eat" buffet. There is a sign by the food that says: "Take what you want but eat what you take." We want it all and fill up our plates with way too much. We are full before the plate is empty. It takes strength to push away the plate and ignore the rule about eating what we take.

It takes even more strength not to get another plate in an attempt to sample everything there is to eat. We don't want to miss having something that might turn out to be wonderful. We have had enough missed opportunities in life and hold the illusion that eating everything will make up for early non-food deprivations.

The buffet of life forces us into consciousness of what we choose and what we pass up, what we consume and what we throw away. It forces us to face the reality that having too much can be as harmful as having too little.

Today I can throw away food without unbearable emotional upheaval. I would rather recycle by giving it away or using it another day but that ideal scenario is not always the reality.

Sometimes I have brought food into my life that no one else needs including me and the choice is between using my body as a garbage disposal or using the mechanical one in the kitchen.

I constantly deal with the old feelings that arise when I throw away food. One thing I know for certain is that cleaning my plate will not feed the hungry children of this world. My monetary donations and time spent helping at a local food bank does more good than eating a whole cake in honor of the starving multitudes.

"Waste not, want not."

That old frugal saying has a new meaning for me today. If I have to keep everything including all my poor choices there will be no room for what I really want in life. My dreams and hopes and goals will be crowded out by the junk.

Wasted food or wasted life—the choice gets clearer all the time.

🍕 The Flip Side of Deprivation Is a Binge

I believed my bingeing was proof that I was bad inside because of my out-of-control behavior. It was as though I was possessed by a monster—a cookie monster. I shoveled in food to the point of feeling sick. I ate lots of kiddie treats—the candy, cookies, cakes and chips that were on my forbidden food list. I ate guy foods—deli sandwiches, triple layer burgers, steak, jumbo hot dogs; heavy foods that left me feeling logy. My all time favorite binge foods were the Greek delicacies from childhood—humus, oily salads, stuffed pastries and my beloved baklava. I ate everything but nothing touched my real hunger.

The end result of the binge was always pain, physical and emotional. My body ached as I awoke from a restless sleep, burping and bloated with a food hangover. My sense of shame was overwhelming. I wanted to wear a scarlet letter proclaiming my sins publicly. I would pledge to never binge again. My eating plans for the days ahead would be a strict diet with all favorite foods banished as though they had left the planet.

Now that the binge/diet cycle is no longer part of my life, I have a much different perspective on bingeing. As I work with hundreds of people who are wanting to lose weight, it has become clear that the binge is a reasonable reaction to deprived ways of eating and living. Deprivation leads to a build up of repressed feelings of anger, sorrow and frustration. Sometimes the eruption of feeling is small and the damage minor. Other times, there is a massive explosion of hot emotions like a huge volcanic spill with damages that need a long painful recovery period.

We can learn to live in ways that don't lead to a build up of emotional pain that explodes in a wild eating spree. A good first step is choosing a way of eating that is humane. So many of us go on diets that are unbearable. Everything we love is out and the amounts are starvation rations. It is a real DIE-it. The goal is to lose the weight fast, have it over and then return to the land of the living. We hate the process and are waiting for the magic day when we can eat everything we want because we want everything.

One of my husband's hobbies is losing and finding the same ten pounds. He's a man of real "will power" and puts himself on a strict diet where he gives up all his favorite treats and cuts his portions to baby size. The weight falls off within a few weeks. I remember his bursting into the house after one of these diets, filled with energy, popping Hershey Kisses™ into his mouth.

"Dolly, I did it. I lost ten pounds. Isn't that great!"

"That's wonderful Alan only why did you buy the giant bag of kisses?

"Dolly, I told you, I lost the weight. Now I can eat whatever I want."

My asking him was a waste of breath. I know what was going on and I understood his need for chocolate as a treat after giving up everything he enjoyed eating. Many people are able to stay in deprivation mode for months before flipping to a binge mentality whether that means having a bag of candy or the entire food park of the mall.

Food deprivation can be subtle. I work for a weight organization with a very liberal food plan, allowing for lots of individual choice with no foods off-limits. It amazes me how many people who join will set up the plan as a diet, eating less than recommended along with excluding their favorite foods and then wonder why they find themselves "out of control."

Sometimes the deprivation comes from our lack of generosity to ourselves while we are in the process of changing to a healthier way of living and eating. When I was bingeing I didn't care how much a box of candy cost but would think ten times before buying mushrooms or cherries and would instead buy day old produce and tasteless packaged carrots. I would get bland mushy fish on sale and end up throwing it away when it turned green in the refrigerator but wouldn't dream of buying the more costly fillet of salmon I adored. It took me a long time to learn to meet my food needs without using bingeing as the only outlet for non-depriving choices. After all, being out of control means I'm not responsible for my expensive wild behavior.

Most of us would go to any extreme if we had a child with allergies who needed special foods or a house guest with specific dietary requirements but when it comes to our own food needs we are often too busy or unwilling to spend the money. It is easy to forget that there are child parts of us living inside who will cry or rebel if we starve and abuse them. Often, when we feel "possessed," it means that a young part of us is running the show. When we are not deprived it is much easier to feel the strength of our wise adult self.

So many of us deprive ourselves unintentionally. A member of one of my classes was describing his frustration over constant evening bingeing. Heads were nodding as he spoke:

> I don't get it. All day long I resist temptation. I eat a piece of fruit for breakfast and avoid the platter of muffins at the office. I don't go out for lunch and munch a few veggies at my desk. I save up my

calories so I can have a big dinner and some snacks at night but always end up eating non-stop once I start.

This is typical behavior for many dieters. It may sound reasonable to undereat in order to be able to overeat but the reality is that the undereating means that now emotional hunger is combined with physical hunger, a force of combustion that is as hard to stop as a speeding train. My class member not only deprived himself of a decent breakfast and lunch but also did not take time out during the workday to socialize with co-workers, an activity he used to enjoy before he started "dieting."

I asked members of my groups what leads them to bingeing. The answers included food deprivation but went way beyond that to other kinds of deprivation from hated jobs to troubled relationships, from boredom to overstimulation and the inability to wind down. Running throughout the comments was the issue of how difficult it is to practice self-soothing without abusing food. The bingeing was often a release from feeling so regimented in many areas of life. "Bad" behavior around food was a relief from the constant pressure of being so "good" in every other way.

My bingeing was always in secret. I felt so bad about my eating habits that I would compensate by either not eating at all in front of other people or just having small bites of diet food. When my sons were little, I would take them out for ice cream cones but never get one. That would blow my charade. I would persuade my kids to have Jamoca Almond Fudge. That wasn't the kind they wanted. They wanted Chocolate Chip or Rocky Road but my favorite was the Jamoca Almond Fudge. My plan was that when the ice cream began dripping, I would say, "Here, let mommy fix it for you." That would be my way to have ice cream without being noticed. Ice cream licks don't count.

I don't think my mother knew what it meant to binge but she was constantly eating. That was the only way she could give pleasure to herself. I never saw my mother buy herself anything special or take a bubble bath to relax. She was driven, driven, driven except when it came to food. Her eating calmed her. Even though she was always cooking and serving others, she did most of her eating standing and snacking as she cleaned up.

My daughter Katie is named after my mother. I hope that she will never be caught in the cycle of the overworked martyred woman. She came home the other day all excited:

Mom, it was very hot at summer school today so I used some of my allowance to have my hair washed. I went into the beauty shop and told them I had three dollars and asked if that was enough for a shampoo. The lady said yes and gave me the best shampoo ever. I feel so refreshed.

Having a shampoo was such a simple thing, yet I understood how it was a big act of self-care for Katie—much more satisfying than a hot fudge sundae. I'd like to think she learned to take care of herself by watching me as I've evolved but she probably got the idea from a friend.

Binge behavior is also about our romance with a fictional version of ourselves as a perfect dieter. We just know that tomorrow we will wake up feeling like a saint able to live off our inner spirit, needing only small amounts of bland food. We can imagine a day when we no longer want sweets, chips or burgers. We see ourselves existing on vegetables, a little rice, an occasional lean bit of protein; shunning cappuccino for the world of herbal tea. Not only will our eating be pure but also our behavior as we are able to achieve great things in the world while maintaining loving people connections. The pounds will fall off us effortlessly as the body of our dreams emerges.

This idealized image may seem absurd but it is not so far from what the typical emotional eater who goes on a crash diet has in mind. The binge can be a desperate attempt to awaken that perfect dieter. When we binge we believe we are being wicked, We hope that if our behavior is bad enough, the good eater within will be evoked. We just know that there is a thin self wanting to come out. Our binge is a cry of desperation to that perfect skinny creature to save us.

While we are eating everything in sight our stress is mounting because we know on a deep level that starvation is coming. We better eat a pound of chocolate, not just a piece, because we might never be eating chocolate again. Soon our meals will be prison fare, frugal and tasteless. We are like animals who must store food in their bodies in preparation for hibernation. Our Sunday feast is the prelude to the Monday diet.

We not only hold a myth of the Spartan dieter in our hearts and we also believe that the reward for deprivation will be abundance without negative consequences. We are like my husband Alan who thinks that once the weight is off, the diet is over and our thinner body will automatically maintain the weight loss no matter how much we eat. We are filled with stress as we are seduced by the opposites of feast and famine, indulgence and deprivation, gain and loss, fat and thin, bad and good.

The anorexic is the tragic symbol of the perfect dieter who has gone too far—the strong willed creature who is willing to die rather than reverse gears and move in the direction of the opposite pole— that place where the compulsive overeater resides. The anorexic doesn't take in nourishment but is haunted by obsessions around recipes, cooking and food. The bulimic is the distorted result of feasting and starving at the same time. The bulimic eats but doesn't keep the nourishment. The bulimic must release what is taken in. The meal of the bulimic is an illusion.

The typical emotional eater knows how to stay away from the extremes enough of the time to avoid serious harm, but anxiety and despair will prevail as long as there is a flip flop from binge to diet again and again and again.

Lynne describes her years of stuggle with bingeing:

My bingeing really went into high gear when I turned sixteen and started driving. I could get goodies all over the city without being recognized. I was anonymous as I ate my way from Sees candy to Kentucky Fried Chicken; from tiny bakeries of every ethnicity to large supermarkets. I would eat until I felt ready to burst.

Then I would go home, strip and stare at myself in the mirror, looking at my distended stomach and guilty eyes. My disgust mounted along with hope that I would never eat this way again. I forced myself to look, eyeball to eyeball, at my most repulsive self so that it would be the final shameful encounter.

I was sure that each binge was the last and that the new day would bring a new me. Each Monday I would start my stringent diet only to go off by Friday with a vengeance.

My bingeing ended when I gave up inhumane dieting forever. I promised myself that the world of food was always going to be open just like the 24 hour supermarket . Nothing was forbidden. It would be about choice not force. I could choose to eat healthy foods most of the time but a poor choice would never again result in my going to bed without supper.

I also was able to stop bingeing by bringing into the present the image of how uncomfortable I felt the morning after. Calling up memories of the bloated sluggish food hangover made bingeing undesireable. The price was bigger than the payoff.

We can set ourselves up for a binge by ignoring reasonable cravings. Sometimes I get a yearning for gummy bears, those chewy kiddy candies that are a dentist's nightmare. If I get myself a small bag and have a few, I'm satisfied and can eat healthfully the rest of the day. If I blow off the craving and start popping carrot sticks, the wanting grows. Soon the carrot sticks lead to rice cakes followed by a sliver of left over pizza or whatever else is around. By the time my food temper tantrum is over, I've had ten times the calories of a few gummy bears and still feel unsatisfied.

Bingeing involves more than eating huge quantities of food. It is also that sense of being "out of control" where feelings overwhelm mind and body. It is as though we are possessed by a creature within who is making choices for us that are totally against what we believe is best. When the emotional storm is over, there is no calm, only shame and guilt. The desire to overcompensate by rigid dieting is understandable but always a mistake.

Learning to set limits without setting them so rigidly that we feel deprived involves trial and error and lots of self-care. When we succeed in making bingeing obsolete, the flavors of our lives become much richer and filling. When we learn to care for our physical and emotional needs, it will not take an endless buffet of food to satisfy our hunger, because we are no longer starving.

🍴 Taking the "Ate" Out of Separate

I was driving past Mel's Diner, a tiny coffee shop with a big sign outside:

YOU HAVEN'T LIVED UNTIL YOU TRIED CHEF REGAL'S COLOSSAL BLOSSOM!

I salivated as an image of a golden french fried onion floated through my mind. I yearned to slam on the brakes and park. Instead, I drove far away without stopping, feeling such a longing and sense of loss. My intense reaction was fleeting, quickly replaced by feelings of triumph, knowing my choice to flee from temptation was a good one.

If we pull ourselves away from a food we want, there are often uncomfortable feelings. We have experienced a loss of a desired object and all our old issues around separation get triggered. We feel very young and exist only in the moment. We forget that gratification of our wants doesn't have to be immediate for our survival.

Separation is part of our lives from birth to death. We are thrust out of the complete comfort of the womb into the bright lights of a new life outside that protective container. We separate from the breast or bottle. People come and go in our lives through circumstance or death. We leave childhood to become adults. We go through many passages in a lifetime, experiencing connection and disconnection over and over again.

Our reactions to the separations in our lives depend on the situation. Our youngest son Robby decides he wants to leave

California and work as a paramedic in Hawaii. It is the first time he will be living far from us. He is feeling excitement about the change. I share in his joy but also feel sadness as it hits me that he is strong enough to leave the nest and fly away. He returns a year later and we are living in the same town once again, but my work of letting go is not over. I must constantly remind myself that Robby is an independent young man, not the little boy emotionally connected to mommy.

It makes sense that we rage and struggle against any separations from the habits and foods that have been a source of comfort for years. In order to let go of the eating habits that no longer serve us, we have to embrace the good feelings that positive change can bring. Leaving bingeing and unhealthy eating behind by graduating to saner behavior can be like accepting a desired job change. The challenges can seem overwhelming but we are attracted to the probability of more satisfying work with better compensation.

One of my members has been a vegetarian for many years. She just returned from a trip to New York, her hometown.

Dolly, you'll never believe this, but every time we went downtown shopping in Manhattan I ate a greasy hot dog from those carts on the sidewalk. I never eat meat and was up all night with indigestion. I just don't understand how I could have done something so foolish.

We talked about it. This was her first trip back since high school and many years had passed. Among her most cherished childhood memories was going shopping in Manhattan with her beloved grandma. They would always stop and buy hot dogs from the street vendor, laughing together as they strolled along dripping mustard on the pavement. Grandma and childhood were gone but the hot dogs were still there, bringing her back to a long lost time, if only for a moment.

If we seek to understand the deeper meaning of our food choices, then we can learn to soothe ourselves in healthy ways rather than waste our energy in self-contempt.

It was a cold rainy day in Los Angeles. I got into my "Little House On the Prairie" mode and wanted to bake cookies. Memories filled my senses of my mother happily baking with me while I licked batter off the spoons. I remembered making cookies with my kids when they were little and the flour would fly as we stirred the cookie dough. I could see the concentration on their faces as they decorated with nuts, chips and raisins.

If I had dared to bake while in that nostalgic mode, I would have been setting myself up for a cookie eating marathon. Instead, I just absorbed the sweet flavors of my memories and decided not to do cookies while in such a vulnerable mood.

It was still a cold rainy day and I had a couple or hours in the house alone. I lit a fire, made baked apples and a hearty chicken rice dish. The house felt cozy. It smelled of cinnamon and chicken. I dimmed the lights and put candles around the living room. It was my new improved "Little House On the Prairie" and it worked for me.

The first time we separate from old behavior around food, the feelings can be intense. It gets easier over time, especially if we attend to the emotional need that the food was filling. On that rainy day, I had to find a way to satisfy my desire to create a cozy country atmosphere so that the separation from the cookie baking would be tolerable.

Sometimes in our impatience to lose weight quickly we separate in a harsh way. We become the parent who weans the baby abruptly, leaving the infant crying much too long. If we go from feast to famine in our eating, we feel primitive and raw like a waiting child. We are unrealistic if we expect ourselves to never want and feel something is wrong with us when old yearnings return.

I try a new restaurant and want the whole left side of the menu. A drive home from work takes me past a beckoning McDonald's and a sparkling ice cream shop. Going to the mall means being assaulted by the smell of cinnamon muffins. I innocently enter the supermarket and pass a line of people waiting for samples of the frozen pizza product coming out of the toaster oven. I know it will taste terrible but want to join the line. There is all this fusion and connectedness around food.

My friend Lynne slips back through the decades to adolescence:

Up until high school I always went to small community schools and felt a sense of belonging. I wasn't a star but at least I was part of the universe. When I started high school everything changed. My neighborhood buddies went from awkward to beautiful and were part of a circle of laughing flirting girls while I was the outsider, chubby and shy—watching them from a distance.

I would get off the school bus alone and head for the drugstore to buy candy bars. As I walked home eating, I felt connected to something. I had a few minutes of relief from the feeling of loneliness that was too painful for me to bear.

My social situation improved the next year and today I am grateful for that year of isolation. I learned to feel compassion for the underdog, for the one who doesn't fit in. Unfortunately, I also learned how to use food as a soothing drug and spent decades separating from the pull of the easy but empty fix. The candy bars never helped other than to buy a few minutes of relief followed by shame. It took me a long time to truly understand that sweetness consumed through the mouth does not soothe inner pain.

Sometimes we slip into food habits that don't have deep emotional undertones. They are just bad habits that come from a normal desire for oral pleasure in the moment. For example, Ron got into the habit of stopping at a donut shop on the way to a class he was taking. The class was fun and he was in a good mood, not needing dessert for emotional reasons. The pastry just looked good and he wanted it.

That donut stop started as a whim that turned into a four times a week routine. Ron knew this was a bad habit and "tried" to stop but his car seemed to drive to the shop on its own.

One day, he arrived just as the donuts came out of the fryer and ecstacy awaited as he slowly bit into the hot hunk of pastry. Much to his shock, he was revulsed as the liquid grease filled his mouth. Ron was haunted for hours by that oily memory. It was the last donut he ever ate.

Once the donut was undesirable, Ron did not have to struggle with separation issues around the donut shop. There was no pain in avoiding something so disgusting. The only pain he felt was the loss of the illusion that the donuts were wonderful. Like Ron, so much of our difficulty in releasing old food habits comes from the false belief that our beloved foods are magical when often they are just a blob of sweetened grease.

My son Aron loves to eat but never has a problem separating from food. Our family was at a Mexican restaurant waiting for our meals. Aron took a few chips, ate them slowly, then peacefully waited for the main dish while the rest of us were still munching.

When his burrito came, he ate with presence, relishing every bite until he was satisfied. He left a tiny piece on his plate. He was done.

Aron wasn't dieting. This is the way he lives. He's a kid who is in the moment, fully invested in what is happening right now. When he eats, he totally experiences the food and knows when he is finished. It doesn't matter how great it tastes or that there is only a bite left; when he is satisfied he separates from the feeding.

Maybe we don't have the physiology of a young active man but the habit of fully experiencing what we are eating can make our separations from food less painful. When we eat standing up in front of the refrigerator or mindlessly snack while watching television or grab something on the run, we don't take in the feeding and remain emotionally hungry. If we diet excessively, we stay hungry for hours or days until the diet ends and the binge begins.

Disconnecting from old destructive eating habits makes separation from emotional eating possible. It is easier to let go of eating habits that keep us from our deeper goals if we can get rid of the illusion that food will fill our emotional hungers along with our physical needs.

We can begin to change our habits by noticing what they are. If we can reserve judgement and just observe, we can find out what is working for us along with what is not. We can solve our problems more effectively if we build on strength. Here are some helpful observations that people in my classes discovered:

> I was surprised to notice that I never overeat at a party. Parties are a passion of mine. I put on something colorful and decorative in spite of my size. I dance and talk to everyone, having a great time. I don't eat much because people are around and it would not be fun to stuff myself and ruin my sense of well being.

When the party is over and I'm home, everything changes. The nice clothes come off along with the make up. It feels like my outer shell is off revealing the flawed me. I live alone and miss the people. I feel disconnected and head for the refrigerator, suddenly famished; ignoring my longing to go to sleep while I just keep on eating.

Another person said:

My experience with parties is the opposite. I hate my appearance and am sure I'm the fattest person there. I'm shy and head right for the food to calm myself. I feel lonely in the crowd. The food eases my sense of being separate from everyone else. Once I get home, I'm safe and all I want to do is curl up in my bed and go to sleep. Food is not on my mind once I'm home.

For many of us, food is used to ward off loneliness and fear. We keep eating so we don't feel a void. Feeling full means we are alive. Hunger of any kind can link us to our fear of death--the ultimate separation from everyone and everything we know. Our expressions around food are often said in humor but reveal our deep seated fear:

Have you ever used any of these common expressions around food?

"I'm so hungry I could die."

"I'm starving to death."

"I'm famished."

"I'd kill for a piece of chocolate."

"I'm dying to taste that."

"It was to die for."

You have probably had the experience of losing someone you really cared about through a move, relationship breakup or death.

You may not have wanted that loss but had to find a way to go on. It is very likely that your feelings hit you physically deep within the body—right in the gut just like hunger pains do. You probably experienced an empty space inside crying out for love as you longed for the person who is gone.

We often get love pains mixed up with hunger pains. Sometimes we experience fury when others leave us even when they are coming back. We want to strike out and damage just as we have been damaged. These feelings can be so unacceptable that we stuff them down with food and end up hurting ourselves.

When we were babies our feedings by breast or bottle were accompanied by the presence of a beloved person who insured our survival. Love and food were one. In the psyche of the infant, when the food is removed the love goes with it.

Every baby must experience some pain around separation but for some of us the loving time was not enough to meet our basic needs and our fixation with this oral stage of early development becomes a life-long struggle. Babies in institutions used to waste away and die when their bottles were just propped up without physical cuddling. It is very understandable that when we go on a severe diet and rob ourselves of both ample food and self-love, we feel like we are starving to death and end up bingeing.

Watching parents feed babies also reveals how our innate ability to separate from food when we are full can be thwarted. So many times the baby will be finished and attempt to push away the food while the parent keeps insisting that the little one take in more. This power struggle between parent and child can go on for years, robbing the child of the ability to respond to inner signals of feeling full. So many of my students and clients say that they are totally disconnected from physical cues of hunger and eat only in response to emotional needs.

We also use the language of mortality to describe fear as in "I'm scared to death." When we are eating emotionally we are often feeding old fears and wounds as the food becomes a lifeline. Unfortunately, it is a lifeline made of straw that cannot support our emotional weight.

Sometimes we fear deep connections to others and find that excess weight becomes a shield of protection. Our weight measures the impact of our bodies on this earth. Big can mean strong, powerful, untouchable. Excess weight can also feel like a prison, isolating us, keeping us from connection.

This lifelong tension between separation and connection is common to all human existence. Desire for oral satisfaction is also a normal part of living. It is vital to understand our human needs so we can have compassion for our struggles as we attempt to stop using food to feed emotional hunger. Self-compassion pushes us gently toward positive change while self-rejection kills the spirit and retards progress.

Every time we separate from something we want, there is grieving and a sense of emptiness. It might last only a few seconds, but is our version of growing pains, to be honored and validated as we make the choices that are in line with what we deeply want in life and separate from the instant gratification choices that bring only short-lived pleasure.

✒ BYE BYE BARBIE

My teenager Katie and I reminisce about the days when she loved to play with Barbie dolls. As she entered her teens and Barbie became an ideal of an image she could never obtain, we would put a few red spots on that clear plastic skin for "zitsy Barbie," mess up her hair for "bad-hair-day Barbie" or pad her stomach for "bloated Barbie"—anything to relax the pressure for perfection that my daughter started experiencing as she absorbed the media images of the perfect female. Katie was adorable but didn't know it back then. She hated her stomach and began to compare herself to the prettiest girls she knew.

"Mom, how come Lisa gets to eat whatever she wants and wear size zero? "

"Why can't I have a flat stomach like Jennifer? I watch her at lunch and she eats twice as much as me."

"Josh asked Robin to the ninth grade dance. I wanted him to ask me. He chose her because she's so pretty."

Katie became a vegetarian who knew her fat grams better than the multiplication tables. Katie was seeking what most females and an increasing number of males desperately want—a "right" body.

I understood her feelings. When I was growing up, my deepest wish was to look like everyone else. I envied the tall thin blonds and hated my short stocky body with full breasts and big butt. I especially despised my round soft belly. I wanted to look like Barbie instead of a prototype for a Cabbage Patch Doll. I was adorable and pinchable but I wanted to be hot and sexy.

Where do we get our body image? I think it starts when we are very young taking in messages from family, relatives and other kids. Later the media propaganda takes over, setting standards of appearance for young women and men that are unattainable.

My best friend taught me the old saying, "Sticks and stones can break my bones but names can never hurt me." What a lie! Cuts and bruises can often heal with medical care but words penetrate deep into the soul and become imbedded there like a tattoo.

I remember second grade and getting teased about being chubby. I can still viscerally feel today what I felt then even though decades have passed. Those old tapes can haunt us so that no matter how thin we get we can still feel fat.

When I was in the sixth grade my teacher asked me to give the spelling test while he went out of the room for a few minutes. Ronny Harris yelled out to me, "Hey smarty, you have a big nose."

From that day on, every time I had to stand in a way that showed my profile, I would cover my nose with my hand.

So many members of my classes struggle to go beyond the hurtful words of others, both from the past and in the present.

Christopher's dad used to call him "Crisco." Mary's sister would taunt her with, "Mary, Mary, two by four, squeezing through the kitchen door." Her father would laugh, colluding with the sister. Carol was called "Hippo Hips" by her cousin. She still sees herself as immense even though she is slender.

When Sue was only fourteen she lost ten pounds. Her mother said to her:

Quick, let me take a picture of you before you gain the weight back.

She did gain the weight back and more as she spent her youth chasing a number that was always just beyond her reach. When she was thirty she lost 97 pounds slowly with a focus on health and lifestyle. She felt great about herself and was talking to that same mother about her success. Her mother with all good intentions said to her:

Honey, that's wonderful—ninety seven pounds! Only three more and you'll be perfect.

This time Sue told our group about her hurt rather than gaining the weight back to spite her clueless mom. Her mother no longer owns the pink slip to her daughter's life.

🗲

Terri is short, stocky and adorable. She was glowing as she tried on a beautiful wedding gown for her sister and future husband. "Oh," sighed her sister, "if only you were six inches taller." Her fiance laughed and agreed. Terri looked at him and saw a future she didn't want. The marriage never took place. Now she only dates men more interested in her insides than her outer size.

🗲

The men in my classes struggle along with the women but they have the additional burden of loneliness. The pain of women and girls to be thin is constantly addressed as voices for sanity attempt to compete with the size zero images that populate the media. Fat men continue to be the brunt of jokes with very little protest from those who would seek a more humane society. The struggle for body love is universal.

I had quite a revelation a few years ago when I went to a high school reunion. The former hunk of the school took me aside to tell me how much he loved to look at me when we were in classes together because I was so cute and pink.

I was certain he must have confused me with someone else. I took a good took at the button I was wearing with my high school picture on it. He was right. I was sort of cute. As for being pink, I probably spent most of high school flushed with embarrassment.

We can't rely on others to make us feel good about how we look. It is in our power to stop the negative self-talk of body hatred that leaves us feeling worthless and hungry, consuming food to deaden the pain.

If I had a small child who was overweight, I would never say to that kid:

Oh, you are so fat and disgusting. You look like a hippo. Get a grip.

I don't ever make spirit-crushing remarks to other people. Yet I never thought twice about going into a dressing room to try on clothes when I was fifty pounds overweight and carrying on a deadly monologue that went something like this:

Oh, you are so repulsive. Look at all those fat rolls. Look at your elephant thighs and blubber butt. And that stomach—you look nine months pregnant.

The tirade would continue:

Look at all those little lines around your eyes. And you're getting a mustache. You need a face lift. No, you need a mask.

I would flee the dressing room and head straight for the food court and it wasn't to get a salad. I would say to myself:

Have whatever you want. Might as well binge. You're so ugly anyway, what's the difference?

Some of the members of my classes believe that feeling bad about their bodies is a good motivator. The reality is that negative feelings might propel us into starting some kind of weight reduction program, but if there is going to be any sustained success, a more positive motivation is needed.

In my groups, we all support one another in taking small and large steps to develop body love. As one of my members put it:

> When I used to look in the mirror, all I could see were two giant thighs walking around. There was no heart, no soul—just two thighs with a big behind attached. Seeing only those parts of myself that I hated was the physical manifestation of a lifetime of the negative messages that almost destroyed me. I have struggled to know that I am more than thighs and butt. I am a human being with needs and the capacity for intimacy, comfort and joy.

We can learn to shift from "out-of-body" living—feeling disconnected, alienated and ignorant of basic hungers to "in-body" living where heart and soul are fused with our physical being . This is a way of life where the appetite for living is stronger than the pull toward the food fix.

"In-body" living means food consumption is not just an emotional process with total disregard for the body. The sensation of food in the body is registered and respected. The body is not pushed beyond physical comfort to relieve emotional pain.

Body-love practices are as varied as the human imagination. One of my friends was dating the new love of her life. He invited her to a beach party charity benefit where the attire was swimwear. She wanted to decline rather than let this man of her dreams see her obviously ample body. She felt she would be in competition with all the gorgeous slim women who would be present at this special event.

She remembered a popular commercial for a suntan lotion called *Bain de Soliel.*® The commercial pictured a tall slender model who was very sexy prancing freely on an exotic beach. My friend decided to imagine herself as the *Bain de Soliel*® woman.

She went to the party in a beautiful bathing suit and a sultry coverup. She never talked about weight or dieting. She did not ask her boyfriend if she looked fat. She just enjoyed herself. It didn't take long before she threw off the coverup and pranced on the beach full of joy. In that moment she caught her own spirit. She released herself from the focus of catching her man or comparing herself to others.

There is a P.S. to the story. She and the "man of her dreams" married and are the beaming parents of twin girls. My friend weighs the same as she did before the wedding even though it still isn't her vision of an ideal weight. However, that old vision is getting dimmer as she enjoys the pleasures of a good life.

My own weight loss and years of maintaining a healthy weight came about as a result of my ongoing journey to love and accept my body with all its imperfections.

I feel grateful for my life. Both my parents died of heart disease. Most of my relatives perished in the Holocaust. I'm short and round like my mother and have my dad's nose. I love the way my body connects me to my family.

I'm still as pink and cute as I was in high school, only much wiser. I have learned to accept the body I was born to have and take good care of it. I began to practice little acts of body kindness while I was losing the fifty pounds and keep adding to my list of simple pleasures.

I often unwind from a busy day with a steaming bubble bath. Sometimes I even light a candle and sip sparkling water from a champagne glass. I gently pat myself dry and rub lotion over my body as though I was my own precious baby.

My style of dressing is unique and always has been through thin and thick. I still get a high from the fun of costuming myself in the colors and styles that reflect my personality.

There is no "right" body. A number on the scale does not measure our worth as human beings. Our clothing size and ring size do not have to be identical. We don't have to be victims of our society's obsession with being thin.

If we don't challenge the obsession, it not only saps our lives but takes down our children as well. Imagine what it does to our kids when we put on an outfit and they hear us wail, "Oh God, I'm so fat," or when we make comments such as, "Stop eating so much. You don't want to grow up to look like me."

Not only do we encourage our children to hate their own flesh but we also teach them intolerance for anyone else who isn't kin to Barbie and Ken. The unthin continue to be the last group openly treated with contempt from within as well as from skinny outsiders. Men don't have the same pressures as women to be slender reeds, but many fat men suffer in silence as they look at the images of the much-worshiped athletic male body.

We can challenge the old ways by noticing when we subject ourselves to inner put-downs and impossible standards. We can engage in small acts of body care and encourage our tiniest efforts.

Katie is now in high school and very popular with boys and girls. She is filled with life—all pink and lovely. Most of the time she likes herself and beams at the mirror. I want to believe that there is hope for her generation. She's planning to get rid of her last remaining Barbie dolls. I like to think of it as the "banish Barbie" game.

⏰ Wake Up!
It's Moving Day!

There's a small park across the street. I love to look out the window of my kitchen and watch the children swinging, gliding, running in sheer delight. Their squeals fill the air:

"See how high I am. I can touch the sky."

"Watch out, I'm coming down the slide."

"Catch me, catch me, you'll never catch me."

The children play, twirl and prance while the grownups sit and talk, getting up only to provide assistance by pushing a swing or catching a flying toddler at the end of a slide.

Once I was the kid chasing waves at the ocean, flying my handmade kite through an open field, playing hopscotch until day turned to dusk. Those years were brief and soon my free play was replaced by physical education where I was the class *klutz*. Wave chasing was out as trips to the beach were for the purpose of sun bathing and flirting, both difficult tasks considering that I was hiding under a towel so my thighs wouldn't show.

When Physical Education ended with high school graduation, I entered the world of exercising and gym joining, both activities high on my "should do but hate" list. I bought every wonder device on the market that promised to give me a body transplant. Nothing worked and those ungainly pieces of equipment soon became rusty hunks of garage litter.

My lifestyle was typical L.A. I drove everywhere and would always park as close as possible to my destination, circling a parking lot endlessly to find the perfect spot. I was on the go all day but evenings were for relaxing with television or reading and, of course, lots of snacks. Getting up to get food was my main exercise. Somewhere inside me there was a child who used to dance with life but I couldn't find her.

When my mother was nine she fell on a wobbly staircase and broke her hip. Her medical treatment was primitive and she ended up with a severe limp. She was full of courage and never let her condition stop her from getting around. She was even able to run with her brother as they hid from the Nazis. I see her in my mind as a plump dervish of a woman whirling in perpetual motion. She didn't drive and went everywhere by foot.

One of my favorite memories is of the day she surprised me by bringing a huge cake to my second grade class for my birthday. She had walked three miles in the hot sun to the bakery and then trekked another mile to the school balancing the cake in her short arms.

Sixty years after her accident, a "miracle" surgery was performed to correct the fused hip. My mother couldn't adjust to the change and never recovered her former mobility. She became dependent on a walker and preferred sitting. Gone was her zest for life along with the zip in her step.

We take our ability to move for granted or see it as another weapon in our weight loss arsenal. Weight control was my motive when I bought a treadmill a few years ago. I just knew that this was the perfect piece of equipment for a new improved me.

I decided to set it up in front of the television and watch a thirty minute sitcom while painlessly exercising. My enthusiasm was high as I hopped on the treadmill and started walking at a rapid pace until I couldn't stand another second. I had lost track of the TV show and couldn't believe that it was still on. My shock was even greater when I looked at my watch and saw that only five minutes had passed. It felt more like an hour. I was done, done and done. Once again, I was a fitness failure.

The treadmill remained quiet for months, an albatross used only for storing laundry. I was through with setting myself up for defeat and knew it was finally time to stop joyless exercising and start joyous moving.

I began by taking a walk outdoors. I left my watch at home and set no goals as to time, distance or target heart zone. My first walk was a short stroll. I even stopped to pick dandelions.

Today I'm still walking for pleasure and hit the road every day. Sometimes I cover miles; other times blocks. My body now craves movement so much that I actually shove the clothes off the treadmill and use it when I'm feeling restless.

Until two dalmatians came into my life, I walked by myself. It was a time to go into a deep place, as I touched the trees and felt my connectedness to the earth. I would stare far into the horizon and watch my problems dim in the vast expanse of the universe. When my mom died, moving was my lifesaver as I would walk and cry and cleanse my spirit.

My routine was early to bed and very early to rise for a morning walk. I would place the alarm clock all the way across the room so I wouldn't be tempted to roll over and go back to dreamland. Often I'd sleep in my sweats so I could take off as soon as my feet hit the tennis shoes waiting by the door.

I still take walks for contemplation but not very often. As our lives change, it is important to be flexible and shift our routines. Today, I'm basically an evening walker and it's a family affair with my husband Alan and our two dalmatians. Every day with few exceptions we take a fast-paced two mile walk shortly after dinner with our canine "kids" in tow.

The dogs spend most of their days in the yard where they romp and bark; at times they pace, other times lie basking in the sun. Their days are filled with routine all revolving around eating, moving and resting. Like humans, they crave affection and are deeply bonded to each other as well as to our family.

Unlike humans, they don't have choices and are dependent on us to be sure they get water, food and exercise. Our yard is spacious but not big enough for two large active dogs. When Alan says, "Wanna take a walk?" they begin jumping and howling in antici- pation.

The dogs are a priority so we rearrange our schedules to make sure they get their evening walk. We can't go as fast as they would like and if we could turn them free, they would be sprinting the two miles, not walking it at our pace.

Looking at animals and children can teach us so much about what is natural to the human species. We can see how indoor cats become domesticated pets whose primary exercise is walking to the feeding bowl, while the outdoor cats spend so much more time running, climbing and chasing, Those dogs who can't romp in a large yard soon learn sedentary ways and often gain weight.

We can learn so much by observing an infant stretching, wig- gling and kicking; or watching toddlers bouncing balloons, splashing in the sprinklers, playing hide and seek, hopping, running, jumping. It's never too late for the child in us to lead our waiting adult to a world of possibilities. We can once again be the kid who moves for joy instead of calorie burning.

We have such an endless menu to choose from: dancing to a soulful beat, taking a hike in the park, chasing butterflies, swinging high to touch the clouds, pumping iron and building glorious muscles, running a marathon, joining a softball league, flying a kite, catching soap bubbles, swimming with the dolphins, strolling on the beach with exposed cellulite, joining a gym for fun, riding a real bike that goes somewhere, stretching and playing with our toes like an agile little baby.

It is important to find what works. My friend Lynne describes her venture into the world of gyms:

I'm a walker and average about a mile every day. However, as I contemplated my flapping upper arms, I decided it was time to join a gym. I hate gyms with their frigid air conditioning, blaring music, sweaty equipment and fast-paced atmosphere. Joining was a "should" that resulted in my hanging out at a place that was a constant stressor.

One morning, I stumbled into a yoga class held weekly at the gym. I was entranced and started attending regularly. The teacher had gentle ways and a soft voice, so unlike the typical loud, hard, driving voices heard in the aerobics classes. She would tell us about her yoga center and how it was designed for spiritual as well as physical conditioning.

I decided to take the bait and try a session at her place. The moment I entered, my insides relaxed. The air temperature was ideal. There were candles, flowers and calming pictures all around the room; the subtle smell of incense filled the air along with soulful sounds of music. The space was peaceful and inviting, a wonderful setting for a blissful experience with yoga.

When my gym membership expired, I didn't rejoin even though the price of renewal was next to nothing. The gym was a good place but not for me.

Today I continue to walk outdoors in nature and go to the yoga studio once a week. On the other days of the week, I spend about ten minutes a day on my own using a yoga tape. The studio is twice as expensive as the same class at the gym, but there is no way to put a price tag on my health and well being.

As for the flapping arms, I bought some inexpensive barbells to work with at home. My arms still look like wings but a few tiny strands of muscles are beginning to be visible. Anyway, wings aren't so bad. Someday I'll fly.

Lynne found in yoga a way of moving that was deeply satisfying; something to enjoy, not just another hated chore in the quest for physical fitness.

I encourage my students to go back in time looking for the ways they used to move with pleasure. Try this yourself. Sit down, close your eyes and see what images and thoughts come to mind as you react to the following question:

When you were a child, what physical play activities did you enjoy most—tag, swimming, riding a bike, hiking, hopscotch, kickball, soccer, softball, skating, snow sports, climbing trees, jumping rope, rolling a ball, dancing, walking around the neighborhood . . . ?

If you patiently start tracking backwards you'll begin to remember something pleasurable involving movement, even if you were a very inactive child. If nothing comes to mind then try thinking back to activities you saw other children doing that you thought looked like fun.

Next ask yourself if any of the activities you remembered could be done today. Usually the answer is yes. If not, then identify some activity you could do today that would evoke the same sense of pleasure.

For example, one of my friends loved Little League as a kid but had no desire to play in an adult softball team. He decided to go to a batting cage a couple times a week and hit a few buckets of balls. That was a perfect choice for him because he loves to connect with the ball and watch it go sailing out in the field. He feels so alive when he is swinging away.

A student in one of my classes used to adore tap dancing when she was a young girl and was excited to find that her local community center has recreational tap dancing classes for adults. She signed up, bought a pair of shiny dance shoes and is having a great time.

Yoga was a good choice for Lynne because as a child she was always drawn to rituals and play that involved no competition or athletic talent.

Ask yourself, "If time, money, age and weight were not a factor, what form of physical activity would I love to be doing?"

If you dig deep for the answer to that question, it can lead you to exercise that will serve the needs of body and spirit.

Wake up, it's moving day! The alarm clock is ringing—time to wake up, get the juices flowing, move and come alive. Moving doesn't have to mean going to a new neighborhood or city or country. Sometimes, it can just mean a stroll down the block.

It doesn't take much for us to get off the treadmill of life and into the playground. Maybe our playground will have a treadmill or exercise bike or even a high tech gym, whatever our personal field of dreams requires.

As for me, my field is filled with winding paths, gnarled shade trees and wildflowers. You might find me power walking, but I'll be chasing rainbows and dogs, not calories.

♥ ♥ ♥ People, People Everywhere . . . Help!

When I first joined Weight Watchers, my husband seemed so supportive. After I'd come home, he would ask eagerly, "So how'ja do?" He cheered when I told him about my terrific first week weight loss. The problem with this happy little scenario was that by the second week the amount of loss was less and by the third week I had binged and gained two pounds. Then the script went something like this:

"Hi honey. How'ja do?"

"Fine Alan, it was a great meeting."

"That's good, honey, but how'ja do?"

"I loved it—very inspiring."

"Yah, but how'ja do?"

It was obvious that he wanted to know my weight loss but I didn't want to tell him because he wouldn't understand. He was a very goal directed guy who attacked a problem with a vengeance and got the task completed. He expected me to come home with a significant weight loss every week and I couldn't deliver.

We had an unspoken contract that went something like this: he would pay for my program and watch our kids while I went to meetings in exchange for my end of it, which was to lose weight steadily and quickly.

This below-the-surface contract was weighing me down with pressure. My goal was to just hang in there however long it took for me to lose fifty pounds. I had given myself a year with the option of longer, if needed.

After several "how'ja do" weeks, I finally said to him, "Alan, stop asking me for a weekly weight report. I promise to tell you each time there is something special, like if I go down a size or lose ten pounds. Then you can buy me flowers or send me a card, anything but a box of candy."

He was initially hurt but went along with my request. As I thought about his wounded feelings, I realized that it wasn't just about the weight. He loves me and never gave me a hard time about my weight until I got him involved. I'm the one who gave myself a hard time and Alan just wanted me to succeed at what was important for my happiness.

He also doesn't like to be shut out of my life. I stopped discussing my weight loss with him but did continue talking about the meetings and let him know how much his taking care of the kids meant to me. That's all he needed. He is like a little puppy dog who requires food, water and lots of affection .

We often get very disappointed if the people in our lives don't give us unconditional love for our appearance and all our erratic behavior around food, even though we don't give ourselves that kind of loving acceptance. We want them to act in ways that please us even when we are so totally crazy-making in our eating habits, not even a psychic could anticipate what we want from day to day.

On Sunday we may be thrilled when our mate comes home with pizza and ice cream. On Monday, we consider the same behavior to be a sabotage of our diet and an act of great insensitivity. We go to a family dinner and aggressively reject the homemade dessert after years of being the biggest fan and wonder why the host looks dejected. We tell our family that we have given up sugar and then are hurt when there is no birthday cake on our special day. We refuse social engagements because we feel too fat to be seen, yet we are ready to leave our spouse for suggesting we lose a few pounds.

Lynne tells this typical story of crazy making with her husband:

I'm a lucky woman. My husband Don eats ugly goodies, those few brands of tasteless cookies and chips that do nothing for my soul. All the tempting treats that entered our house were brought in by me until the day that traitor came home with honey dry-roasted cashew nuts, one of my favorites, There they sat in a clear glass jar in full mouth-watering view each time I opened the cupboard, which was at least ten times a day.

Don would take a small handful once in the evening while I was popping them hourly. Finally I begged him to hide the nuts. He agreed. The next day when he was away I went to the cupboard for cashews only to find they were gone. Muttering under my breath, I began to tear the house apart looking for them and was furious when poor Don arrived home, an innocent man totally unprepared for the wild-eyed woman who pounced on him demanding the cashews. He explained that he was trying to be helpful by taking the nuts to work, but had one more jar in the car. He looked totally bewildered when I made a frantic dash outside to retrieve the nuts. When that last jar was finished he went back to his old habit of bringing home oily peanuts which I hate. That's my nutty version of living happily ever after.

Are other people really sabotaging our efforts? Do they actually spend sleepless nights and endless days plotting ways to keep us from lean clean behavior? If the people we put into our lives are jealous, petty, mean-spirited and downright nasty, it's possible. It is more likely, however, that the people around us are just doing their thing oblivious to our constantly changing food needs. They would probably be willing to be helpful if we would let them know what that would mean, and issue updates when we change the rules as often as our clothes.

Ask yourself these questions:

- What behavior do I want from the people in my life?

- How can I clearly make realistic requests for that behavior?

- How can I show appreciation of any efforts in the right direction?

- How can I handle those times when other people don't want to grant my requests?

- What can I do for others so that the support goes both ways?

Grappling with these questions will give you a starting place for getting clearer about your needs from a cooperative position that takes the other person into account.

Consider this example of what not to do:

You are at a dinner party at the house of a good friend. The friend does not know you are on a healthy new food plan. She brings one of your favorite desserts and starts to serve you a piece. You look at her with fire in your eyes and angrily say, "I can't eat that. Get it out of my sight. I'm trying to lose weight." Or you smile and in your most passive little-kid voice say, "Oh, I just love that but I shouldn't. It's so fattening." She urges you to enjoy yourself and have some. You quickly give in and feel betrayed by your friend for being a food pusher.

Let's consider some possibilities of what you could do in this kind of situation. If the host is a good friend, you can call ahead and discuss your dietary changes, offering to bring a fruit platter. If calling ahead is not for you, then get skilled at the tactful but short refusal of unwanted food from a place in you that is solid, not open to persuasion. Something like:

"That pie looks delicious but I'm going to pass tonight. I'm totally satisfied from the wonderful meal you served."

Another option is to simply say:

"No, thank you. I'm going to pass. "

True thin mentality people have a way of saying no that doesn't leave room for messing with them. They aren't rude or loud but give a clear "no" that comes from inside where their values live.

I have a size zero friend who loves food but has the stomach capacity of a gnat. She will come over for dinner and rave about everything while eating only dollops of a few items. She always gets excited over dessert but pushes her plate away after one bite because she is full. She isn't dieting, just in flow with her food needs. I've never seen her pressured by anyone to eat more.

Clear communication is not just about food. Many of the feelings that lead us to the refrigerator for edible therapy come from interactions with others where we didn't get our needs met. When I passed the oral exam for my counseling license after a rough time of it, I left this message for a friend who wasn't home. "Hi, it's Dolly. I passed. Please call me back and say, 'Yippee!'" When she called back, she delivered the exact message I longed to hear, leaving me feeling terrific.

We can't expect others to be mind readers. If your partner has never brought you flowers, don't wallow in hurt; communicate what you want. Go to your boss to ask for a raise if you believe it is time. Tell friends your restaurant choices rather than seething when you end up somewhere that specializes in fried fat. Let your kids know the rules before you freak out because they are not following them.

We are not always going to get what we want from others. It is possible that what we are asking is not in harmony with their wants and needs. Our friends and family can get burned out from our changing food regimes and won't always want to go along with our endless requests. That doesn't have to stop us from going forward with our goals. At least by being clear about our needs and putting it out there we increase the odds of getting what we want.

People were always talking me into eating rich foods or having seconds because I was so wishy-washy inside about what I wanted. If I was on a deprivation diet, which in the old days was often, I secretly wanted others to push me to eat. When they did, I could blame them and avoid facing my own lack of clarity about my choices.

It took me a long time to stop involving other people in my eating either as food police, watching to make sure that I didn't overeat or as food pushers who knew my weaknesses and could always count on me to eat on demand. I didn't believe I was capable or worthy of being in charge of something as basic as my own food consumption.

I used to feel such shame about my weight and eat lots of rich foods alone, in hiding; convinced I was the only one who did that. Like many of my students, constant closet eating caused me continuous anguish. I would keep a box of candy in the freezer for unexpected guests. Each day I'd take a piece or two and then rearrange the spacing of the remaining pieces so that my eating would go undetected. When the box was almost gone, I'd run to the candy store to replace what I had consumed. These food shame games were a painful part of my daily existence.

There were so many embarrassing incidents. I still cringe remembering the time when my husband was out of town for a conference and the kids were sleeping overnight at friends' homes, leaving me with the house all to myself. I decided to have an oreo orgy. I filled the bath with steaming water, lit a candle and put a heaping dish of cookies on the tub ledge so I could consume the delicacies while luxuriating in the bath. I was in a state of bliss, back in the womb, when a loud voice broke the spell:

"Hi honey. I'm home. The conference ended early."

Footsteps were coming my way. I quickly put the dish of oreos under me in the tub. My husband came in bearing kisses, so happy to see me. I tried to match his enthusiasm but was not succeeding. He began to look at the bathtub and wondered why the water was dark and murky. I made up some explanation about my new bath oil beads and felt immense relief went he went off to sort through the mail.

These kinds of experiences seem very funny now but at the time they were moments of shame, not just over my eating but also over the deception that went with hiding my behavior. I wasn't breaking the law or doing anything wrong, yet I felt like a criminal just waiting to be busted.

After too many years of this kind of hidden life, I decided it was time to come out of the closet and eat in the open. The first time I ate dessert in front of my friends at a restaurant I kept waiting for lighting to strike my plate, but nothing happened except an incredible feeling of liberation.

In my days of using food as a drug, it was as though I was in a coma, constantly doing for other people whether it was good for me or not. Everyone loved me but few knew me. I often felt lonely among people because of my hidden eating. Taking care of others kept my feelings of self-contempt at bay. When I emerged from the coma and started taking better care of myself, the new improved me was not always welcomed with open arms. It took time and lots of adjusting as my husband and friends dealt with the real me, not the people-pleasing shell of myself.

One of the biggest changes I made was getting rid of self-contempt. We teach others how to treat us and I was through with being good natured about hurtful comments, even those made with caring intentions. As long as I hated my weight and constantly made sarcastic remarks about myself in front of family and friends, I couldn't blame them for echoing my words. When I came from a place of self-dignity, people treated me with respect. If not, then I forced myself to speak up and let others know it was not okay for them to make unwanted comments on my weight, eating habits or character.

When we see people around us as out to sabotage, we are left feeling disconnected from our support system. This feeling of being alone even in the midst of family or friends is very common for anyone who eats in secret and gets into the habit of avoiding intimacy for fear of being found out. If we get mad at lots of people and turn away from them, then we can safety continue to feel disconnected and apart, old familiar feelings.

We can shift perspective, seeing our friends and family as similar to us, imperfect human beings with a desire to love and be loved back. Then we are in a position to work out the problems we have with others from a win-win place where there are no villains, just a bunch of little kids in grown up bodies trying to get along.

If we are on a path of change where getting thinner means a transformational journey, there may be a few people who go by the wayside. Hopefully, it won't be a spouse or other family member. Usually losing weight through a holistic positive program strengthens family ties because we feel so much more loving from the inside out. As we become more compassionate about our own imperfections, we have a greater tolerance for the imperfections of those around us.

At the heart of it all is love—giving it and getting it back. Lynne tells this story about her mother who loved to feed people as a way of showing how much she cared.

My mother was too old to prepare the lavish dinners of my youth but was in heaven when any of her children or grandchildren would come to visit and head right to the cupboard where she kept a huge stash of sweets ranging from candy to fresh baked goods. I used to be her favorite customer until my eating habits changed. She tried to understand but it hurt to see her fallen face when she couldn't give me anything yummy to eat. I would hug her and explain that my visit was about being with her, not her food. That helped for about five minutes and then she would check again to make sure I didn't want a little something. She continued to stock the cupboard week after week just in case I changed my mind.

One day when I came by, she had just made chicken soup and offered me a plate. My eyes lit up over the array of cooked vegetables in the steaming broth. Within a flash, I had a heaping plate of soup flavored carrots, celery, onions and parsnips. My mother was in her glory, feeling useful and young once again. Each time I came, her little apartment was filled with the aroma of chicken soup and my plate soon runneth over. She also gave me a doggie bag of vegetables to take home along with cookies for the family. She wasn't a saboteur, just a generous person used to garnishing her love with food.

If we think of our dealings with people as opportunities to give and receive love, it will be so much easier to handle the frustrations and disappointments in human interaction. A major reason why we long to lose weight is social. We want to love and be loved. Pushing others away only increases our loneliness. We can also be a positive force for changing the negative attitudes in our society toward heavy people if we treat ourselves with respect and teach others in our lives to do the same.

Remember Forever . . .
Count It As a Vegetable and Move On

I purchased one of those 96 loads, 300 fluid ounces, "easy to use" laundry detergent dispensers. It was a peaceful Sunday morning as I trustingly followed the directions on the container for activating the one load-at-a-time release mechanism, and left the house to run errands as the washing machine was starting to fill with water.

Upon returning home, I noticed a swimming pool size puddle in the entry way coming from the laundry room and flowing toward the living room carpet. I was now in the middle of my own *I Love Lucy* real life sitcom surrounded by 2.34 gallons of thick slick soap that came from the now empty "easy to use" dispenser. There was detergent wherever I looked. It spread behind the washing machine, dryer, and every corner—everywhere. I was in shock without a clue of what to do next.

My first instinct was to start with the kitchen, specifically the cupboards where the chips and licorice sticks called my name in seductive tones. Fortunately, I decided to go with my second instinct which was to begin the clean up. I took old towels in a futile attempt to sop up liquid. This accomplished very little other than to cover me with soap.

After fifteen minutes of my less than stellar efforts, Alan arrived home from a meeting wearing his new three-piece suit. It was a "chief paramedic to the rescue" moment for him as he started to kneel down to help me. As soap began to travel up his pant leg, he realized that no lives would be lost if he changed clothes first. Soon my hero of a husband came back wearing swim trunks; his arms were loaded with a dozen rolls of paper towels, rags and buckets. He sprang into action moving the washer and dryer, mopping, wiping. Together we were quite a team going from towels to mops to rags, using hot water and cold water from buckets, pots and pans. Finally, the mess was cleaned up with pockets of detergent debris still left in the little crevices beyond our reach.

When it was all over, we took showers (not together). I watched the suds fill the stall from my slippery body that was covered from head to toe in soap. So much for the "easy to use" dispenser. The kitchen was still slippery so we decided to go out for dinner. Once we got out of the house, sat down and relaxed, we looked at each other and burst out laughing. We laughed all night. I wasn't even tempted to order a bunch of rich foods to sooth my jangled nerves. The laughter was more fun than dessert.

I never thought consciously about "count it as a vegetable." The veggie perspective occurred naturally as I handled the situation. It was my fault that the dispenser was set improperly but the error was unintentional and very human. I did not get into my old ways of berating myself for being stupid and then eating over it. My efforts were totally directed toward the "moving on," which was the clean-up.

Alan can sometimes be blaming but even he has been influenced by my non-shaming philosophy and didn't get into his old stuff of rolling his eyes and asking accusingly what could have possessed me to let such a calamity occur. He didn't even freak out about the soap on his new suit.

The relaxing dinner filled with laughter was our way of letting go of the mess and enjoying the calm after the sudsy storm. We also will do whatever it takes to avoid a repeat of our little "soap opera."

As for me, I'm back to putting in the soap by hand and have dispensed with the dispenser.

So much of our eating is over the little stresses in life that seem overwhelming at the time but mean very little later down the line. When we get into bad feelings about ourselves we stay in the acute pain of the event way too long and often turn to food to soothe that pain. If we let go of endlessly berating ourselves, then we can go to the "move on" phase where the mop up begins as we problem solve and do what we can to make things better. Maybe there will be some residual mess but it won't be as bad as the consequences of wallowing in shame and guilt over the past without moving forward.

My life is always filled with "count it as a vegetable" moments, both big and small. A huge challenge for me revolved around the trauma of passing the oral exam for my counselor's license. After going back to school to get my master's degree and putting in two years collecting three thousand hours of experience, I was ready to take the board exams.

The first was a comprehensive written test. Not being a champion test taker, I studied night and day and took a prep course. Luck was with me as I passed on the first try. Now all that was left between me and my license was the oral exam. Just thinking about it terrified me.

My friends and students told me my worries were for nothing because if anyone would be good at an oral exam it would be me. They went on to assure me that my speaking skills were great and I'd ace the test. Their confidence only increased my anxiety because they didn't understand about these orals. This exam was not a personality contest where I could charm the test examiners. The pass rate was only around fifty percent. The test involved just one hypothetical counseling case that was to be thoroughly dissected with over a dozen specific points covered in a discussion of diagnosis and treatment.

My fears must have been premonitions because I failed the test the first time round, missing by a margin of one little point. There was a six month wait to take the exam again. This time I was slightly more confident, believing that the law of averages along with my extensive preparation would work in my favor but it was not to be. Again, a no-pass by one point.

Now I was in such a state of stress that I missed the application date for the third exam and had to wait eight months for a retake. My self-confidence took a nose dive while my weight was on the rise. I dealt with my emotional state in therapy and talked about my overeating in my groups until finally I began to get a grip.

I stopped eating over my feelings and did everything possible to make the third time a winner. I invested lots of money on prep courses and individual coaching. My buddy Lynne did a hypnosis visualization with me for relaxation and success. I took *Ginkgo Biloba* to sharpen my memory and bought a bracelet of red power beads that was called *Success.*

I bathed with a perfumed bath oil called *Tranquility* and got weekly massages to melt away my stress. I bought a new outfit to wear on the day of the exam, had my hair done and my eyebrows waxed. I even ate fish the night before the test because someone on TV said it was a good food for memory. My breakfast on the morning of the test was a protein power bar. I was as ready as humanly possible and finally let go of my need for control and released the outcome of the exam to the universe. What would be would be.

We can only do what we can do. We can't control outcomes, only our attitude and behavior. My goal meant a lot to me but finally, after much suffering, I made the decision not to be so attached to the results and more into the moment of the process.

I still cared about getting my license and was not about to give up my efforts to make that happen. What I did drop was the frantic energy attached to the outcome of one exam. My trust in the vision of myself as a licensed psychotherapist remained strong. I just needed to keep going and be patient.

My experience was another version of "count it as a vegetable and move on." I wasn't counting my big dream as a vegetable. I was releasing all the shame around not passing the first two orals mixed with desperation about the third test, a combination that was driving me to the refrigerator. It was only by letting go of self-contempt that I was able to study and get mentally prepared for round three.

It was also about "counting as a vegetable" my wanting to be in control of the outcome even though that was an impossibility. The grading of the exam was not in my hands. My challenge was to have faith in my ability to handle any test outcome. That meant I could relax and enjoy life during the weeks until the results were sent out.

I did pass on the third try and it was a thrill to take my place as a licensed therapist. However, the victory was somewhat anti-climatic. I was already a winner by the way I dealt with defeat and deepened my resolve to let nothing stop me from doing the work that is my true calling in life.

You have experienced many tools for dealing with emotional eating. "Count it as a vegetable" can be the one that reminds you to get out of endless rumination over the past. Let those words be an invitation to dust yourself off and move into the present where change is possible; whether it be change of perspective, attitude, behavior or all of those. Let "move on" encourage you to be a constantly evolving person, going toward a higher quality life for you and those you impact.

Let this be a time to replace your "shoulds" with a vision of a way of living that reflects your divine self. A "veggie" perspective is good for you—kissed by the sun, nourished by the rain and rooted in the rich earth.

"Count it as a vegetable and move on" is the heart of our message to you as you release yourself from the food-abuse/ self-abuse cycle.

SECTION TWO
How to Lose Weight and Keep It Off

This section, written by Lynne, reflects the conviction that both of us hold about the importance of a holistic way of eating and living. We want you to understand the major parts of what we call the "Circle of Health" and know how each one can impact your life.

People can lose weight sanely and keep it off while enjoying life at the same time. You can be one of those people. This section will tell you how.

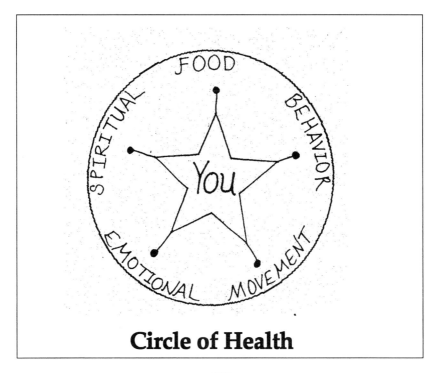

Circle of Health

✌ Making the Commitment

Let's look at the first part—losing weight. Losing some weight is routine for many of us. I've lost hundreds of pounds if I can count the ten pounds I've lost and gained over and over again. Losing all the weight we want is a different story, especially if what we want is based on fantasy not the reality of our genes and jeans. Here are some typical motives for losing weight. Notice which ones are true for you.

- **To be more attractive**

  This is the most common reason for starting a diet, especially among the young and young at heart. This motivation can range from a desire to be in a healthy weight range to an obsession with the media's version of the ideal body. It can go all the way from self-improvement to self-annihilation.

- **To be socially acceptable in the personal and work realms**

  Many of us believe that what we weigh determines our popularity, ability to hook a mate and our power in the workplace. We are filled with visions of how the thinner self will go on to find love, respect and success. We always feel at least ten pounds away from bliss.

- **To be healthier physically**

  This is often the goal for any of us experiencing physical problems from excess weight or unhealthy eating habits. This motivation also includes healthy people who worry about the future impact of their present eating habits. When the number of our age increases along with the number on the scale; anxiety about physical survival increases.

- **To be healthier emotionally**

  Some of us believe that losing weight will be a character transplant where we will emerge thin, beautiful and filled with self-confidence. We are hoping that old feelings of shame and guilt will disappear with the unwanted pounds. This motivation ranges from a realistic desire to free ourselves from constant emotional eating all the way to an idealized image of becoming a person free from all struggles with temptation.

  ❂

You probably recognize bits of yourself in all the categories. The pull to lose weight is usually a combination of moving toward what is desired along with moving away from all we hate about our weight and eating behavior.

Our strong motivations are what make losing some pounds possible on any weight reduction scheme. Both the sane and crazy plans produce partial results for most of us. It is the second part—keeping it off—that involves ongoing change and commitment.

Dolly and I hope this book will empower you to lose weight now and never find it again. It's not fun to be a human yo-yo. Compassionate ways of eating and living are much more satisfying than hanging on to old habits that keep us frustrated.

This section of the book will promote weight loss if your weight is beyond what is physically good for your body. The ideas in this section show you how to banish behaviors that keep you from reaching and maintaining an optimum weight. If you are already at a healthy weight, you can learn how to stay there without constant stress as you navigate in a world mined with food.

I have studied successful weight loss programs for over twenty years by doing research and working for weight organizations. My private counseling practice has included individuals and groups dealing with weight issues. My deepest experience has come from my own intense struggle to stabilize my weight and tame my wild eating behavior. Everything in this section comes from the blood, sweat and fat grams of my life as a former prisoner of emotional eating.

My journey has led me to the common sense conclusion that the best way to lose weight and keep it off is through a holistic approach that impacts every area of living. We can go beyond the superficial process of picking a "diet of the month," dropping some weight and then either gaining it all back or living in a joyless state of deprivation.

A symbol of wholeness is the circle. Think of a holistic way of relating to food and life as a "Circle of Health." Gently put yourself inside the circle. Surrounding you are the elements you need to be at a healthy weight all of your days. These include food plan, exercise, behavior modification, emotional support and spiritual practice.

The circle is a continuous flow of one life force energy into another in an unbroken line. Sometimes you will feel centered as you draw sustenance from all parts of the circle. Other times you will be pulled more to one or two parts and lose that sense of centeredness.

For example, you may be starting a new food plan and feel as though food selection and preparation is taking over your life. At other times you might feel totally disconnected from the good eating plan you vowed to stay on. You are not "off your diet." You are just pulled by other aspects of the circle that are not about eating.

It can be both empowering and emotionally soothing to know that you can still be within a ring of health in those times when your outward behavior around food and exercise is light years away from your ideal. That may be when you turn to sources of emotional and spiritual support for help. You never have to be out of the circle if you make the choice to get in and stay.

A circle is a continuous line. If you take a pencil and draw a circle, you'll find that the starting point of the drawing is also the completion point. The "Circle of Health" works the same way with each aspect of health-giving energy flowing into the others. So when you meet food needs you can also be meeting spiritual needs. When you get emotional support, your eating habits can change. Getting physical exercise can increase your internal well being. The circle doesn't have rigid boundaries that confine. The outer rim can expand as you grow and change.

In this section of the book we will look together at the major elements of this life-giving circle. Let your deepest desire for transformational change guide you to make a strong commitment to finally end the food-abuse/self-abuse cycle and embrace the "Circle Of Health."

Your Food Plan

If you want to lose weight without losing your spirit you need a way of eating that touches every part of your being. Our earliest human contact was around feeding when we were newborns. If we are still getting up every day with no clue as to how to feed ourselves and thrive, we go through the day with a deep longing to be taken care of physically and emotionally.

Choosing a good food plan is a big step toward meeting our primal need for survival. If you want to lose weight, the ideal plan will be at a caloric level that gives you a safe rate of weight loss--2 to 8 pounds per month as a general guide. Your fantasy weight loss is probably 2 to 8 pounds per day. The turtle in the old Aesop fable really was smarter than the hare by knowing that slow and steady is the best route to the finish line, much quicker than the fast start that ends up off the path.

Unless your weight is physically killing you right now, a fast weight loss is just a devil's contract with a gain back guarantee clause in the fine print. On a healthy plan your rate of loss will depend on your starting weight, what you were consuming before beginning the program, amount of exercise, personal metabolism and the idiosyncrasies of your body.

The calorie range for a healthy weight loss plan is typically between 1,200 and 1,800 per day. A good plan gives you most of those calories from fruits, vegetables, whole grains and protein. It will also include small amounts of unsaturated vegetable oils and some milk products. It will be flexible enough to accommodate specific needs due to food allergies and health problems. Information about vitamin supplements will be included.

A good food plan is based on the best nutritional and health information available. Expert opinions about the amounts that are ideal for each food group shift like the wind, so you will need a plan that has enough flexibility that you can flow with the changes and make some decisions yourself about what is best for you.

Gravitate toward a plan that is a love-it not a die-it, one that includes a variety of colors, textures and taste sensations. The portion sizes of the basic foods will be humane. If your total meal would fit better on a saucer than a regular plate, you're probably starving even if it is a saucer of steak topped with whipped cream.

A humane plan will fit a variety of lifestyles and eating preferences including use of convenience food, restaurant eating, having several mini meals as well as the traditional arrangement of three main meals and a few small snacks. It will be a way of eating that doesn't isolate you from others.

The plan will account for about eighty percent of your food choices, giving you the security of guidelines for most of your eating. There will be a twenty percent window of opportunity to add those foods you love that don't offer much for the body but feed the soul. This is where chocolate and other passions come in. No foods are off limits unless you put them there. The limits are on amount and frequency. Joy is not excluded.

A good food plan teaches a way of eating that satisfies physical hunger and nutritional needs. This leaves "only" emotional hunger to deal with and that is where the other elements of a holistic plan come to the rescue.

Remember that even the most liberal of healthy food plans take work and effort to follow, especially in the beginning. You will be learning new skills such as taking time to buy and prepare some of your food, making time to sit down and eat, expending effort to find new foods you enjoy, as well as other changes that will be needed.

Your eating plan should not feel hard as in hardship and hungriness. It needs to pass the test of a "yes" answer to the question: "Can I eat this way forever?" If the answer is negative, then you are just on another diet that will leave you feeling like a loser of much more than a few pounds.

Finding a plan you can stay on forever means paying attention to what is important to you other than losing lots of pounds. If you are only connected to the desire to be thin, then you are prey to every diet plan that blows into town, as if you were a leaf tossed about with no true place to touch down.

You can find out more about what is important to you in a food plan by asking yourself the following questions:

- What foods do I believe are vital to my health?

- What foods are so high on my pleasure list that I don't want to eliminate them?

- Do I thrive with lots of structure in a plan or do I want only a few guidelines with lots of freedom of choice?

- Do I crave volume and need the feeling of a full stomach?

- Is taste more important to me than volume?

- What types of foods have I consistently craved over the years—

salty, sweet, soft baby type food, crunchy chewy food, hefty meats, vegetarian food, etc.?

- How much time am I willing to spend on shopping and food preparation?

- What does my intuition—that deep place of knowing inside me—tell me about what to eat for my highest well being?

These questions will get you started in forming your values and recognizing your needs so that you will be more likely to choose a forever food plan. When your values and eating plan don't match, the result is usually to dump the plan.

In my diet days, I was frequently choosing ridiculous diets that featured foods I didn't like. I would go on liquid meals even though I'm the kind of person that will always take the orange over the orange juice and hate the bloated feeling that comes from blended shakes. Of course, I never lasted on any liquid plan even if the drink was just at breakfast. I was a sitting duck for any craziness that promised fast weight loss whether or not it made sense to me.

Most of us wouldn't dream of letting a stranger determine our value system about honesty, safety or lifestyle but will follow the advice of a diet guru without a second thought. Our desperation is worthy of our compassion but not the state of mind from which to make important choices.

Spending time on the answers to the questions about your eating values can help activate your thinking process. The following exercise can help you connect with your deep knowing about what is best for you:

Find a comfortable quiet place to sit and relax. Close your eyes and take a few deep breaths. Now imagine you are in the presence of a very precious child who happens to look just like you only younger. Feel deep love, free from judgment, for this beloved younger version of yourself. Now lead the child to the table for a meal prepared or purchased by you, a meal designed with your child's health and well being in mind. Remember that children need enjoyment as well as nutrients. What will you give this child? Make this meal a loving pleasant time for you and the child. You can eat, too.

Spend as much time as you want imagining, using as many of your senses as you can. Make it a movie in your mind with color and sound. When you are finished, open your eyes. Notice your thoughts and feelings now and in the next few minutes.

Whatever you did or did not do with this exercise is fine. You can do it again and again and even go through a whole day of feeding your imaginary child. If you have real children of your own, you may find that they are living your ideal "diet", one planned by you with love for their health and well being. How you feed them or anyone else you care about will give you good information about what is important to you.

It is possible that some of you went into guilt melt-down when I painted the rosy picture of how lovingly you are feeding others. Maybe you are an overworked parent who uses the local hamburger joint for constant take out and settles the kids in front of the television with a bag of junk food so you can get a moment of peace. A home-cooked meal might be a microwaved frozen pizza. If this is you, rather than dissolve into guilt, just notice lovingly what you feel guilty about and it will lead you to the kind of eating you really believe is right for you and anyone else you are feeding. Guilt and shame can be teachers instead of executioners.

Anything you can do to connect deeply with your values around food and eating behavior will help you gravitate toward a plan you can live with for all seasons.

Maintaining weight loss on a value-based way of eating simply means adding a little more from the major foods on the plan—an extra piece of bread, a larger portion of protein, more fruit and vegetables. You would maintain your weight by continuing the healthy eating that brought about weight loss. The high calorie emotional foods would remain a small percent of your total eating. The ideal plan would also give you lots of ways to recover from those very human bouts of excess without gaining a lot of weight.

We don't want to give you an exact food plan in this book because that would be like giving a teenager printed instructions for driving a car. You need the support of live instruction. Most of you already have a sense of how to lose pounds. You know the foods and amounts that are keeping you from a healthy weight. Knowing and doing are not always partners, so outside support for working the food plan is crucial. Just like the baby cannot survive without being fed by a parent or caretaker, we need personal assistance in our early stages of learning how to eat and nourish ourselves.

There are several places to get a good food plan without going bankrupt. Dolly and I have both used a major weight loss organization to help us lose weight and keep it off. It is one of several commercially available organizations that promote food plans based on sound health principles. Medical centers, universities and wellness centers are also good resources for weight loss programs that include support. HMOs often provide wellness programs including weight reduction. I've been on the staff of an outstanding weight management program that is offered by a large HMO to both its members and the general public.

Another source of a food plan is to work with a registered dietitian or health care provider who will see you on a regular basis and design a well-balanced program based on your health and personal preferences. Make it a priority to have a comprehensive physical so that you are aware of any allergies or medical conditions that need to be considered in your choice of foods.

There are other resources for good plans including a few of the celebrity-based plans that come with audio tapes, video and internet support. Dolly and I prefer live support systems but recognize that some people do fine connected by web.

Be discriminating as you sort through the choices available to you. Don't let desperation lead you to charismatic quacks offering the quick fix. Tear up those ads promising you instant weight loss in one easy product. It will come with a hefty price tag financially and emotionally. Choosing the plan that will help you lose weight and keep it off forever is a monumental act of self-care. You are worth it.

☺ Behavior Modification

Behavior modification is a great way to lose weight and keep it off by changing habits rather than focusing on a specific food plan. The "rules" of behavior mod are based on what researchers have learned from studying noncompulsive eaters who stay at a healthy weight without dieting.

Many of the "eat whatever you want" weight reduction plans are just a set of habit changes that will almost always cause calorie intake to go down regardless of food choices. The power of behavior modification greatly increases when used along with a healthy food plan, exercise and other elements of holistic living.

We have woven behavior modification into every part of this book so that you have constant support from us as you take small and big steps of change. This section will teach you three very powerful habits of behavior change put into an easy-to-remember phrase: "Sit down. Slow down. Size down."

Sit Down:

So much of our eating is guilty, hidden, standing up, on the run, in the corner, walking in the mall, tasting while we cook, grazing around the kitchen—everywhere and anywhere but rarely in a chair at a table.

Even if you are not going to eat at a table, sit down, sit down and sit down! You deserve the dignity of eating like a human being, able to acknowledge that nourishment is being received into your body. Sitting down is calming and brings you into awareness of the food you are consuming. Let yourself eat like you are royalty—a king or queen, anyone but the court jester.

Eating sitting down is always an improvement over standing up but there are levels of quality to our sitting behavior. Eating in a movie theater, in front of the TV or in the car is sitting down behavior but not in the spirit of focused caring eating.

Take the time to sit down at a table for most of your eating, with real dishes and silverware, even adding candles and flowers now and then. Use a nice placemat or tablecloth. If you are eating at work or someplace where you can't control the environment, pick the best setting you can find. Be your own guest of honor at the table.

If you want to increase the calming effect of sitting down when you eat, say an affirmation or prayer before beginning to eat. You don't have to be religious to engage in spiritual practice around food. Blessing your food can give you a moment of pause that calms emotional hunger. You can use a blessing that is in the spirit of your tradition or just take a moment to slow down and calm yourself before beginning to eat.

Blessings and affirmations may seem awkward at first but over time most of your eating can become a gentle receiving from the bounty of the universe, not a guilty act of indulgence. Do not expect yourself to eat with calm and dignity all the time because that isn't realistic. Sometimes we want to be wild animals. Just aim for enough change to make a difference in your behavior.

Remind yourself to sit down by posting sticky pad notes all over—at home, work and in the car. If you find yourself eating standing up, don't get upset; just lead yourself to the closest chair.

Remember that it takes time to change a habit so be kind and patient. Eating sitting down is a practice you will learn to love because it feels good and will make the process of weight control much easier. You can learn to enjoy sitting down and eating with loving care.

Slow Down:

You have heard this one before and have probably tried it only to give up in frustration. Most efforts to slow down are doomed because we are trying to slow down way too fast. It's like the jarring feeling you get if you suddenly slam on the brakes of your car. That isn't something you are going to want to do on a regular basis. Slowing down starts with sitting down so that you can relax your body. It is hard to slow down when you are standing, running or hiding.

Going back to the car analogy, think of your present rate of eating as miles per hour with 35 miles being the ideal speed. I used to be a very fast eater. I equated my reckless eating speed to 80 miles per hour. What number describes your typical rate of eating? Whatever you come up with, attempt to reduce your eating speed by 5 to 10 miles at a time so that you barely notice the difference. You are just chewing a little longer, waiting an extra beat between bites, taking time to swallow your food. It takes about twenty minutes for the brain to register that you are full. You will feel satisfied with less as your eating time lengthens.

If you slow down in small increments you can get pleasure from the relaxed feeling that comes with slightly slower eating. Every few weeks you can reduce your eating speed until it is at a safe rate. You are no longer speeding, but not going so slow that it is crazy making.

Another way to derive enhanced enjoyment from eating is by going into slow motion when you are eating a high calorie beloved food. For example, if you want candy, buy one piece of your favorite kind and sit down at a table. Then instead of speed swallowing, take small bites and savor the flavor, letting it touch the tip of your tongue where the taste buds for sugar are highly concentrated.

Using our driving analogy, you have entered a below average speed zone for just a short period of time so you can lengthen your pleasure. Going into slow motion for a few minutes is a pleasant challenge. Doing this all the time is agony.

When possible, eat with other people and take time to socialize. Pause in your eating when you are talking or intensely listening. Do what you can to avoid angry meal time conversation because that will rob you of pleasure and stimulate emotional hunger. If you are eating alone, try having soothing music in the background.

Slowing down is an opportunity to eat with awareness and lengthen the pleasure we derive from eating.

Size Down:

Sizing down is a challenge because there is a child part of each of us that resists limits and wants what we want when we want it with no boundries. The adult parts of us know better and want to behave in ways that are good today and tomorrow. The words "size down" reinforce our desire to size down in weight by reminding us that eating less can give us more of what we really want in life.

If you can embrace slow steady weight loss rather than an overnight body transplant, it will only take a little sizing down of food to lose weight. Taking in less food can occur in a variety of ways. One effective practice is by eating just as you always have but cutting the portions slightly at each meal or snack. If you eat just a little less consistently you can lose weight without feeling deprived. You will barely notice that you are consuming smaller portions.

Another way to size down is by keeping portions generous but having less of calorically rich foods. Instead of a piece of apple pie, you have a baked apple. You discover low fat salad dressings and sauces that you love. Finding satisfying low calorie foods takes effort but the results are worth it because you can eat generous portions and still lose weight. We are not talking about substituting massive amounts of veggies for everything you love. Carrots won't satisfy a craving for carrot cake. The spirit of sizing down calorically is to find alternates that are close in kind to the food you are choosing not to eat.

A third way to size down is by dealing with those motley pairs that we adore—the "gruesome twosomes" food/behavior combinations that often result in lots of unconscious eating of rich foods. See if you relate to any of these:

- Eating while watching TV

- Eating and reading

- Eating at the movies

- Eating and driving

- Eating while talking on the phone

- Eating and shopping, etc., etc., etc.

Our eating is linked to the activity and we respond automatically like the dog who comes running at the sound of the can opener.

Cutting down on these pairs starts by becoming aware of them and then making a choice to either go cold turkey and eliminate the eating behavior or else cut back so that the habit is not a problem. The first way is initially painful but often ends the habit within a few weeks. The second way is much slower but a good choice if you want to limit, not end, the habit.

In my own life, eating and TV watching was a big source of overeating so I decided to stop the behavior totally. It was crazy making for a short time but then got radically easier. Without the food, television wasn't so enjoyable and I started to do other things. Today, over twenty years later, I still don't have any desire to eat when I watch TV. I'm like the rat in the laboratory experiment who went down a path in a maze that led to cheese. The cheese was always there and the path was always taken. And then one day there was no cheese. The rat was distressed and kept trying the familiar path until it soon became clear that the cheese was never going to be there. At that point, the rat stopped going down that cheeseless road.

I love to read and eat. This used to be a big problem and I was not willing to eliminate the behavior. The sizing down occurred when I reduced the frequency of the habit by changing the rules. Instead of the "all you can eat anytime you read" policy, I decided to combine reading and eating only when sitting at a table with a planned amount of food. After that food is gone, the eating is over even if I'm not done reading.

In the midst of much grieving, I gave up my favorite gruesome twosome of eating while curled up in a chair reading a novel, an old habit that soothed my frazzled insides but came with a huge price tag that landed on my thighs. Now I only read and eat at breakfast and when I have a small evening snack at the kitchen table.

Reducing frequency helps us size down but we are still involved with the habit and there will be those vulnerable times when we go back to the old excessive behavior. I rarely have a problem when I read and eat at breakfast because morning has never been a big eating time for me. However, the evening snack can get out of control if I'm feeling stressed and using eating and reading to relax.

You can use a variety of ways to size down. It helps to say the words "size down" several times during the day, both out loud and internally. Use a loving voice that entices you to make this positive change.

Making behavior changes is a process that takes practice and ongoing support. Reading this section over and over and over again can make the habits come alive for you. Use the positive suggestions of "Sit down—slow down—size down" as a reminder to treat yourself like a human being. Don't get mad at your vulnerable self when old habits seem stronger than new ones. Let these behavior modification practices lead you to a gentler more pleasurable way of eating and living. Think of your new improved habits as elegant eating—slow, sensuous, satisfying. You are learning to eat with awareness rather than unconsciously using your precious body as a dumping ground.

Food Diaries:

In my research on successful weight reduction plans, I noticed that all of them encouraged or required some type of food diary daily or periodically. Some of the charting was just a list of foods consumed. Other diaries included feelings and a variety of observations about behavior.

If you have chosen a food plan that comes with live instruction, it is likely that you will be given some kind of a form for recording food choices, along with the encouragement you'll need to get in the habit of doing this helpful behavior that most of us approach with massive resistance.

The food diary is a great tool for increasing awareness of what, when and why you are eating. If you charted everything you ate and did nothing else to lose weight, that habit change alone would probably result in weight loss and saner eating because unconscious eating would be eliminated. It is very difficult to write and be unconscious at the same time.

Hypnosis:

Hypnosis is another way to modify behavior. It starts with relaxing mind and body, which helps soothe the hungry beast within who gnaws at us relentlessly. Ongoing relaxation practice can have a major impact on reducing stress based "out of control" eating.

While in the relaxed state you can just be calm or you can use imagery to create your vision of how you want to live. When you are relaxed enough, the critical intellect goes on vacation, leaving you in deeper contact with your unconscious mind. You will be open to positive suggestions as well as able to rehearse in your mind the way you want to behave around food. You can get a picture of yourself looking slimmer and healthy, feeling confident. Athletes do this kind of mental training regularly to improve performance.

There are excellent commercial audio and video tapes available that can give you opportunity to use relaxation and imagery for general wellness and weight loss. Many health centers and universities offer classes that teach a variety of relaxation and imagery techniques.

Affirmations:

Use of affirmations modifies behavior by changing thinking as you repeat over and over statements that support your highest good. It is a way of wishing in the present tense so that you begin to believe in your wishes and act upon them. Your thinking moves from idea to action, from head to heart.

The affirmations in this section will help you end the food-abuse/self-abuse cycle. I have given these to students for years and have many testimonials about the way in which these simple statements were a huge source of encouragement.

Make copies to place around your house, including the refrigerator and at least one mirror. Carry a copy with you to have whenever you need a boost of positive energy. Add your own affirmations to this list or change these in any way you want. Here they are for you to use and reuse.

SLIM SENTENCES FOR DAILY DIGESTION

- **I choose to lose weight now.**
- **I eat slowly, taking in less and enjoying it more.**
- **I prefer foods that are low in fat and high in nutrition.**
- **Everything I eat contributes to my health and well being.**
- **I am human—capable of poor choices along with good ones. My goal is to be slimmer, not saintly.**
- **I can increase my positive actions by asking myself: "Will this choice better my life?"**
- **I can change because I love and value myself as I am now.**
- **Taking care of myself enables me to be of service to others.**

Affirmations, food diaries, hypnosis and learning new eating habits are all part of Behavior Modification—all part of a holistic way of eating and living in the comfort of the "Circle of Health."

Movement

Watch the progression of healthy human development by observing a growing baby. In the earliest stages, that little one likes being swaddled in receiving blankets as if still in the womb. Within days the need for tight holding gives way to an expanding array of free movement. Within a twelve to eighteen month period the typical baby goes from the confines of the mother's body to enjoying the sensations of walking, running, skipping and jumping. No one has to tell an infant to get up and start exercising. It is as natural as breathing.

If you are struggling with your weight and constant emotional eating, you might feel more like returning to the womb than spreading your wings and flying. Unless you are a very athletic person who loves sports almost as much as food, you may shun anything that resembles exercise.

Exercise makes the body come alive. If we hate our bodies, our unconscious wants us to avoid anything that makes us aware of bodily sensations. We don't want to work up a sweat, feel a beating heart, flushed face, tingling muscles. We don't want to do anything that is good for our bodies because to do so is to acknowledge that our less than perfect physical beings exists.

The benefits of exercise make it worth going beyond deep resistance to find ways of moving that work for you. I used to think that the only reason to exercise was to burn up calories, and would grit my teeth as I tried to undo excess eating by working it off. Calorie burning does happen, but rarely at a level that makes a difference.

The big benefit of exercise is health and well being along with increased body awareness. Constant dieting can produce a sluggish metabolism that doesn't burn up calories normally. Ongoing physical movement can aid metabolism and lower the set point—that place where the body wants to stay even though it may be higher than desired for health and appearance.

In my work as a psychotherapist, I see how exercise can help with depression. Vigorous movement produces endorphins that are like a magic pill to elevate mood states. This becomes important in a holistic weight management program because it is so much easier to control emotional eating when we feel calm and content. There are often feelings of depression when we give up old ways. It is comforting to know we can use movement to lift our spirits.

What exercise is good for you? The answer to this question takes some trial and error. If in doubt, start with walking. Walking can do wonders to produce good feelings inside and out. So can other forms of movement that impact the whole body such as swimming, dancing, yoga, karate—to name just a few.

Our chapter in the first section of this book—"Wake Up! It's Moving Day!" can help you choose a physical activity that is right for you.

Dolly and I can be your emotional coaches as you get started because we really understand both the agony and ecstasy of going from sedentary living to being physically active.

I used to hate anything that resembled exercise. Now I'm addicted to walking and rarely skip a day. This has nothing to do with will power. Exercise is not a "should" in my life anymore even though that's what it was for years. Now moving is a part of the

"Circle of Health" that nurtures me and keeps me secure even on those days when my eating is way off base.

No matter what your physical or psychological barriers to an exercise plan, let yourself get started. Get support as you seek to be more physically active. Most good food plans include exercise information. You can also enroll in a class, get a trainer, find a walking buddy, use tapes, join a gym—whatever you need to get going.

Not all exercise has to be purely physical. You can benefit from using meditation practices that focus on breathing and mental imagery where you visualize yourself in states of health and well being. Any practice that increases your body aliveness and awareness will help get you moving. I've recently become hooked on yoga for health and flexibility. It also brings me into deep states of peace and harmony.

Regular exercise that feels healthy will make it easier for you to make good food choices because your respect for your body will grow. It isn't just about weight loss but about gaining a sense of care for our bodies so that we will want to eat in ways that contribute to the quality of our living.

♥ Emotional Support

It is easy to be an emotional eater. We are always having feelings and are constantly in the presence of food. You don't have to be a psychological wreck to get joy or relief from the primal process of eating. It doesn't take much to go from occasional misuse of food to harmful overeating in response to feelings.

The best way to modify emotional eating is with emotional support. You are turning to food to deal with stress, suffering, boredom, as well as to accompany the whole array of happy feelings. It makes sense that the way to handle years of strong associations between internal states and comfort eating is by developing strong links of non-food support that can stand up to the power of the food fix.

Live people support is crucial. Ideally, you have chosen a food plan that comes with a person or group that will help you deal with emotional eating. There are also 12-step programs that focus on compulsive eating behavior, offering frequent meetings and individual sponsors. Universities, adult education programs and community health centers are good sources for classes and groups.

Both Dolly and I are therapists. We believe in the value of taking an hour out of your hectic week to sit down, stop the world and go inward. Inner journeys are not encouraged in our culture and often kept secret by those who take them, so they will not be viewed as emotionally weak. We believe it takes strength to be willing to heal emotional wounds and find ways to live according to your vision and values.

Find a qualified therapist you like and respect. Let that person be your witness and guide during this time of change. Good therapists can be found at all financial levels from expensive professionals to community clinics offering a sliding scale.

In addition to counseling, you can learn so much about handling your emotions from articles, books, tapes, videos and even the internet. We wrote this book with the hope that you will use it for more than information. We want our words to offer you support as you move out of the food-abuse/self-abuse cycle. We have unzipped our outsides and exposed our insides because we believe that revealing our trials and triumphs will ease your journey. We hope you will read and reread the words that are meaningful to you so that the ideas get deep into your bones.

This is a good time to keep a journal as an outlet for your emotions, dreams and challenges. Use words or pictures to go deep inside yourself. You can just get a blank book and begin writing or use a manual on journal writing to get you started.

Another crucial source of emotional support is family and friends. It may take our loved ones time to adjust to our changes, but if we don't turn away from our inner circle of people or expect them to be masters of sensitivity, then they can be of help in ways that can make a difference.

For example, a thin family member who doesn't care much about food may not understand your eating issues but might be willing to stop bringing home foods you are trying to avoid. A caring friend who has never dieted can still be a good listener as you talk about stress in your life. Remember that your changes will impact others as well as you and most of us struggle when our world starts shifting.

Using food to meet emotional needs isn't all negative. You could think of yourself as a magical person because you know how to take an edible item and transform it into an adventure of passion with every bite. Only an eater-type can get excited about breakfast, lunch and dinner. Emotional eaters are often optimists because they can always look forward to the next meal.

We need help when that emotional connection to food becomes a tight grip that pulls at our lives, impacting the size of our bodies, keeping us from peace of mind.

My weight has stayed in a healthy range for over twenty-five years. The thirty pounds I lost isn't a huge amount, but considering all my problems with bingeing and other compulsive eating habits, it seems like a miracle. I have never been willing to follow any food plan perfectly and still have some bad habits. The reason I've been able to keep the weight off all these years has nothing to do with will power. It has to do with my total willingness to get help when I need it.

I have my times when I'm disconnected from my chosen food plan and start gaining weight. When that happens, I get support right away by calling an understanding friend, discussing what's going on with my therapist or going to a meeting sponsored by a weight organization. Sometimes I do all three. I know how easily a few pounds can become ten or twenty.

If we try to hang tough until the out-of-control eating stops we can do lots of damage. Don't go it alone when you are overwhelmed by your feelings. There is help everywhere. When we let shame over our behavior keep us from getting help, the consequences can be very hurtful.

It is so soothing to be on a holistic plan like the "Circle Of Health." Much of our despair comes from the pain of being on a diet filled with hope in the beginning only to come off it with a thud along with the sinking sensation of having failed again. There is no failure when your program is a circle. The food plan is only a piece of the whole. There is always some place to connect. You are always part of something bigger than your human imperfections.

🌿 SPIRITUAL PRACTICE

Our spirit is like a pilot light, providing the underlying power for our energy. When we are constantly off and on diets, unhappy about our bodies, feeling damaged and defeated; it is our spirit that suffers. We feel as if we have lost our way. We feel singled out with an affliction that seems so unfair—prisoners of bodies that feel heavy and alien. Our lives may look successful on the outside but on the deepest inner level we are weary and longing for peace.

It is through spiritual living that we can go beyond the tyranny of an ego that insists we look a certain way even if that is not our destiny; an ego that demands behavior changes that push us into desperate choices that never work.

It is vital that a holistic weight control program include spiritual needs. Spiritual growth and practice is what elevates our existence; without it, the task of losing weight and maintaining that loss seems futile and empty.

Our spiritual needs are on two levels. The first is centered around the personal—capturing our own spirit—finding meaning in life. There is often guilt, conscious or unconscious, about spending time on the primitive need of food consumption. You may find it hard to accept that precious moments must be spent every day on intricate details of what you eat and how you eat it. This can feel selfish in a world filled with starving, suffering people.

The counterbalance for the necessary self-preoccupation as you heal the food-abuse/self-abuse cycle is to spend enough time engaged in living that has deep meaning beyond the self.

There are many ways to find meaning in our lives including work, home, community service and the arts. These are places where you can flourish, whether it be in just one of those areas or in all of them.

Ask yourself: What are my talents, passions, values? How can I contribute and make this world a better place? Where am I needed? How can I best use my energy? Where must I say "no" so that I have time to say "yes" to what really matters? When do I feel most alive? How can I spread love in this world? How can I "feed" others once I'm no longer starving?

The wish to be at a healthy weight, free from food obsessions has at its core our desire for peace of mind and feelings of worthiness. You will elevate your sagging spirit by making the world a little better by the work you do, the child you nurture, the charity you serve, the talents you share with others; your kind words, hugs and smiles.

The second level of our spiritual needs goes way beyond our personal journey as we let ourselves be open to connecting to the vastness of the universe; that place where we are just a speck; where weight, eating habits and accomplishments are insignificant. We are transported beyond our egos when we connect with the mysteries of the universe.

I recently traveled to Maui. Every morning there would be a bountiful breakfast buffet overflowing with foods of all kinds. Most days I would choose wisely, enjoying the tropical Hawaiian fruits topped with yogurt. A couple of mornings my choices were more decadent and those old feelings of shame crept up from somewhere deep inside.

After breakfast I would walk along the beach, stopping to take in the power of the ocean, the endless waves, soothing sounds, a light breeze. In those moments of connection with nature the breakfast was forgotten, the shame gone as peace washed over me like a wave. In the presence of the infinite space of ocean and sky, concerns about the extra fat grams, how I looked or what I weighed evaporated in the morning mist.

When I was recovering from breast cancer surgery, I worked with a healer who gave me assignments to help deepen my spiritual connection to the universe. One assignment was to go outside each night and look at the moon. For the first time in my life, I learned about moon cycles and could "see" light even when the moon was not visible. Looking up at the sky was very much like watching the ocean. My troubles, even the big ones, seemed so small in the unending space of the galaxy where peace surrounded me.

Nature—sky, ocean, mountains, streams, flowers, earth—open us to the natural world where we have a place; where our individual concerns are not so heavy. The arts can also soothe and connect us to deep places within that awaken us spiritually whether we are making art or taking in the creativity of others. Meditation is another way to go beyond the critical self into universal realms.

Religion and prayer are powerful sources of spiritual well being. Connection to a higher power can bring peace and sustenance. Worship in the presence of a community can ease loneliness and offer many kinds of support. That community can be within a specific religion or a spiritually-based group not connected to organized religion. It can also be a 12-step program where release to a higher power becomes a foundation for healing addiction.

Spiritual practice leads to inner peace, freeing us from a bottom-less hunger that no amount of food can satisfy. As we become more spiritually evolved, the restless yearning wanting inside is soothed.

Impatience with the size of our bodies eases along with the frantic search for the magic diet that will get rid of lots of pounds fast. When restrictive dieting ceases, bingeing also stops. Once you view yourself as a cherished child of the universe, obsession with physical appearance ends.

That churning inside that leads to wild eating flows into calm when body, mind and heart are in harmony. Spiritual connection strengthens us internally, increasing our ability to triumph over temptation. When we lose our spiritual way and are overcome by emotional needs, our language reflects that lost self:

"I was out of control."

"I don't know what possessed me to eat like that."

"Once I started, I just couldn't stop."

"All my good intentions went out the window."

"It was as though someone else was in my body, doing all that eating."

Those words reflect a sense of being in the grip of alien forces that go against our true values. These forces may seem to come from some outside source but are actually the needy parts of ourselves that work against our highest good if we don't deal with them.

The inner struggle against outside temptation is not about will power. Will power is used in our language to mean forcing ourselves into extreme behavior that doesn't leave room for compassionate existence. It takes deep self-love to resist instant gratification and seek higher desires.

Our food temptations plunge us into a struggle with the desire to go for momentary relief no matter what the future cost. We are tempted by the lure of a "devil's contract"—pleasure now in exchange for pain later. In order to triumph over the forces that keep us from reaching for our stars, we need inner calm and connection to something bigger than ourselves. It is crucial that our spiritual needs be identified and met. The forces of temptation are too big for us to handle without the larger perspective that universal connection provides.

Spirituality is not just an aspect of the "Circle of Health." It is free flowing energy that fills the circle. Our spiritual practices can elevate our existence as we see ourselves as part of the divine expanse of universal energy.

SECTION THREE
Our Stories

You have experienced bits and pieces of our lives in the chapters of this book. Now we want to let it all hang out so you will know that we haven't just been giving advice. We want you to see that we have lived through the trauma of the food-abuse/self-abuse cycle and used every principle of change that we write about to transform our own lives. We want you to know us and understand how the compassion we bring to your struggles comes from our own experiences. We hope our stories will give you hope and increase your confidence as you courageously go forward and make your dreams happen.

☯ Lynne's Story

My weight issues started in the womb. My previously slender mother gained forty pounds during her pregnancy because she doubled the amounts of everything the doctor told her to consume—just to be on the safe side. I was born premature, an underweight moment in my life that unfortunately was never documented with pictures. By the time the first snapshots appeared I was already a chipmunk-cheeked babe with fat rolls bulging out of my diapers.

My childhood was spent surrounded by good cooking and ample portions. Money was tight but food was a major priority. A drive out to a root beer stand in the countryside near my hometown of St. Paul was cheaper than most other forms of recreation and sipping root beer floats was pure bliss. Having friends and relatives over to meet and eat was my parents' favorite way to show caring.

My mother equated a full table with a generous heart and she and my father provided both as I grew up surrounded with huge portions of food and love. And when love wasn't enough to change a frown into a smile, food was brought in to soothe the wounds of living. My family tree was filled with big stomachs and big appetites. The cup was never half empty or half full. It was a given that all cups and plates were to be overflowing in good times and bad.

In my mind, I was a fat kid and a fatter teen. In reality, my size would be categorized as plump rather than obese. I was never an outcast and had lots of friends, all of them thin. My size was big enough to warrant shopping in the Chubby Department. Getting pummeled by snowballs along with taunts of "fatso" was a typical winter event in the boy-laden neighborhood of my young life.

One of my least happy childhood memories was riding the bus on the way to camp wearing the required shorts, only to notice in horror the slim legs of my bus partner. Her bony thighs took up a few inches of space while mine were soft hunks of dough that spread themselves all over the linoleum-covered seat. I kept praying no one would notice. I wanted to disappear.

In my teen years, the teasing stopped but by then my inner bully was strong and the words I hurled at myself were crueler than any of the taunts of those long gone little boys of my childhood. The big boys were much kinder. Sometimes I even had a date, but my Saturday night dance card was often unfilled and then my date was the edible kind along with foods that were much more exciting.

The overt teasing ended but I had to endure insensitive comments from my skinny friends who could not understand why I had a weight problem. They never saw me eat anything but salads and an occasional tiny piece of fun food.

One of my worst memories probably never happened:

My family took me out for a birthday treat at a popular ice cream parlor. I looked around, saw no one familiar, and ordered a hot fudge sundae. When it came, I scarfed it down before anyone could see me.

The next day I was reading an article in the paper written by a prominent columnist who was commenting on the problem of fat teens. She wrote that on the previous evening she had been at a well known ice cream hang out, sipping tea while observing behavior.

It was there that she saw an overweight teenage girl out with her family, ordering a huge hot fudge sundae with whipped cream. She went on to preach about self-control, noting that the sundae was the last thing that teen should have been eating.

I was sure then and believe to this day that she was talking about me even though there were dozens of ice cream parlors in town, all of them serving hot fudge sundaes to teenagers. I wasn't able to let go of the embarrassment for years and still feel pain now remembering my reaction to the article.

I lived a double life, a good gregarious kid to the outside world, a shamed weak-willed failure on the inside. My family didn't have a clue. Each of them was also pleasantly plump, but in their eyes I was perfect as long as I remembered to send thank you notes to relatives. My mother was an overeater who would diet from time to time, but was off more than on. Unlike me, she never tried the self-contempt diet. Her feelings about her body were healthy. She dressed very stylishly and couldn't understand why I hung out in black pants and overblouses.

Teen years took me from the blissful childhood days of ordinary overeating into the decadence of a world filled with fad diets, bingeing, crazy food schemes, breakfast skipping, lunch skipping, diet pills, and despair over my less than perfect body. Those years also took my family from St. Paul to Los Angeles, the land of the blond babes in bikinis. At least, I was sort of blond with only occasional help from a bottle.

In spite of my inner turmoil about weight and food, I was a good student, an excellent speaker and had a nice circle of friends. I was an optimist, certain that instant transformation was around the corner, if only I could find the right street.

In the spring and summer when high school days ended and college loomed ahead, that transformation did occur. For a period of five months, I focused every bit of my will and energy on eating sanely; no skipped meals, no bingeing and no pills—just three moderate meals and a few snacks of fruits and veggies. I was following the food plan guidelines suggested in this book only I didn't know it. I also knew nothing about holistic living and toughed it out alone. I did have support from my parents who knew better than to even try to dissuade me from dieting, even though they were worried that I'd get too thin. I think they never got over the trauma of my premature birth.

By the time I started U.C.L.A. my skin was clear and my body was slim. I was indeed the butterfly who emerged from a cocoon to a better world than my days in the dirt as a caterpillar. Being thin and sort of pretty was everything I hoped it would be even though my date card was still occasionally empty and no Hollywood producers came calling. What did occur is that I felt good inside and out. I loved looking in the mirror because that young woman looking back at me was smiling and had dancing eyes, thrilled about life.

I remember standing on the top of a huge outdoor stairway that separated one level of the campus from another. I stared down at the buildings and people below and said to myself, "I'm thin, pretty, young and smart. The world is mine. If only I could put this moment in a bottle and hold it forever." Actually, I did bottle that image in my memory bank and take it out whenever I need a shot of confidence.

My twenties were a decade filled with teaching, marriage to Don and motherhood. On the weight front, the story was somewhat bleaker. My resolve to live life as a thin woman was strong but I didn't know how to maintain my weight loss. I thought that once I was thin, I could eat whatever I wanted without a problem; that my body would magically keep me thin just as it had kept me fat.

I descended into a pit of compulsive eating that was especially horrendous during my college years and early days of teaching. I was either dieting or bingeing, desperate to get a grip on my eating. I would often fast on Monday to undo the damage of the weekend. Days of studying would be accompanied by chips, soda, candy, pizza, popcorn. If bulimia had been a household word at that time, I probably would have gone that route. Luckily, it never occurred to me to throw up as the way to have my cake and eat it too without wearing it.

I became a teacher at a school far from my home, which meant very early to rise and a return of my old high school habits of skipping breakfast. Lunch was an apple gobbled down as I ran around the classroom doing things for the afternoon. I got home exhausted and famished. Dinner became a long meal that started standing up at the refrigerator in the late afternoon and ended in front of the TV as I relaxed and graded papers, the relaxation coming from the exquisite pleasure of hand to mouth gratification, feelings numbed as my mind guided my non-eating hand over the endless mound of papers.

I left teaching in my late twenties when I became pregnant, vowing to eat better now that there was another depending on me for life. I didn't really understand what to do other than cutting down on junk food and making friends with vegetables. Becoming a full time mother determined to feed my child and husband decently did lead me in the direction of healthier food habits.

However, staying at home with our baby daughter meant I was constantly involved with cooking, feeding and an open refrigerator door. I began to gain weight at a slow but steady pace resulting in an extra ten pounds that wouldn't budge.

By the time I was pregnant with our son four years had passed and my ill-fated attempts to lose ten pounds had added almost twenty more. That last twenty occurred so fast that no one noticed except me. I was teaching Parent Education classes part time, a very active mother and constantly feeling pressured. My old food habits of meal skipping and bingeing returned. I was like an undercover criminal in my ability to hide food and sneak-eat. Black pants and flowing overblouses along with slender hands maintained my semi-slim image. I was wearing maternity clothes as soon as I found out I was pregnant because nothing else fit.

The pregnancy was an incredible blessing. After more than two years of trying to have another baby, including visits to an infertility clinic, my husband and I accepted that our daughter Carol would be our only child. Now there would be another and I wanted to be worthy of our good fortune.

My doctor was concerned about my rapid weight gain and wanted me to go on a healthy eating regime that would be good for the baby but would also keep my weight gain down. I was determined to follow his advice and finally learn how to eat right— whatever that meant. My young brother had just lost eighty pounds on Weight Watchers and started working for the organization. He urged me to join and I reluctantly agreed.

I still remember the night of my first meeting. On the way over I stopped at the liquor store for my last fix, three of my favorite candy bars. I arrived with chocolate on my breath.

The meeting room was overflowing with people. I was embarrassed to be there and wondered what I could possibly have in common with those fat folk drinking diet soda and opening cans of green beans. These were the early days of Weight Watchers when it was common for members to be snacking on low cal food during the meeting, a practice no longer in style today.

The meeting finally started and my resistance melted as I heard so many stories of small and large triumphs over years of bad habits. My sense of not belonging evaporated and the scene felt like a family reunion. These were my people and I was inspired. If the woman sitting next to me who had been fat for decades could lose over one hundred pounds, surely I could follow the generous food plan for pregnant women that was handed to me.

Four months after our son Rob was born, my weight was back down to where it was at age eighteen after my first successful weight loss spree. Only this time I had spent a year not just a few months eating healthfully, changing behavior patterns and enjoying the immense comfort of a support group. A year of good habits left me feeling confident that I was ready to keep my weight off on my own. Wrong!

The next several years were busy ones with family, part time teaching and my new venture, going back to school as the first step toward becoming a psychotherapist. My life was good enough but there were always the ups and downs which for me meant using food to deal with my feelings. It was hard for me to see myself as an emotional eater but as I got deep into the study of psychology and started going to therapy, it became impossible to deny the ways in which food was my drug. The constant snacking served as a twenty-four hour feeding tube taking the edge off my feelings. I didn't recognize the food-feeling link in my life because I never stopped eating long enough to feel anything.

Shortly after finishing graduate school I went back to Weight Watchers, this time with only a few pounds to lose but eager to return to a healthy way of eating and stay connected forever. That's when I starting lecturing for the organization to keep myself on track while giving back to others. I didn't recognize it then but the combination of food plan, support group, therapy, and my newfound interest in exercise put me on a holistic path of eating and living that is the foundation of this book.

The next several years were filled with counseling, giving workshops, working for Weight Watchers and being with my family. I continued to eat healthfully most of the time and was as much at peace about eating as I ever expected to be. I was finally exercising and could even feel an occasional bud of a muscle.

One of the jobs I had with Weight Watchers was a management position where I interacted with members and staff throughout the whole city. I literally had contact with hundreds of people, many of them long term members at goal weight who seemed to shoot down the popular belief that people who lose weight gain it back. These long term success stories included weight loss that ranged from ten pounds all the way to a staff member who lost 255 pounds and kept it off for over twenty years. Some of these people lost it fast, others slowly. They came from all walks of life as well as a variety of ethnic and socioeconomic groups. They had one thing in common. They kept on coming to meetings, initially to lose weight and then as lifetime members checking in at least once a month. Many of them joined the staff so they could inspire others and be motivated to stay connected themselves.

As a manager traveling to meetings all over Los Angeles, I witnessed firsthand how the power of support is so vital for long term success. It was the same phenomenon typical of friends and clients who were in 12-step programs. I was to see it again in later years as the Behavior Modification teacher for a holistic weight loss program, Freedom From Fat™, at Kaiser Permanente Medical Center in the San Fernando Valley. There is nothing like hanging in there and just showing up—a crucial part of continuing to maintain healthy behavior around a substance whether it be food, drink or drugs. As one of my teachers put it, "You have to do it on your own, but you don't have to do it alone."

In 1993, something happened that had a great impact on my life, including my relationship to food—a diagnosis of early stage breast cancer requiring major surgery. I was struck by an intense sense of protectiveness toward my body unlike anything ever experienced in my past. From somewhere deep inside came a knowing that I would never ever again put anything in my mouth that did not contribute to my health and well being. This inner jolt was different than the millions of times I resolved to give up junk food. My fierce determination to survive led me to a whole new view of my body as a holy temple to be treated with love and respect.

I entered a period of eating that seems like a dream today, an altered state that brought me to a new consciousness. Out went meat, cheese, white sugar, white flour, hydrogenated fat, saturated fat, salt and all preservatives. I changed from shopping at the supermarket weekly to a daily pit stop at a local health food store to obtain freshly squeezed wheatgrass and other supplies for the day. I became the health food nut that was the brunt of my old jokes. My stash of vitamins and magic potions cost more than my wardrobe. My previously beloved desserts looked lethal to me as though they were labeled with a skull and crossbones like the iodine bottles of my childhood.

For the first time in my life, I experienced what it was like to eat healthfully and joyfully at the same time. Nothing stood in the way of my new value system. In my travels, I found that even greasy spoon restaurants would usually have wheat bread, lettuce, tomatoes, onions and mustard so I could make a big sandwich. This was not deprivation because a sandwich represented liberation from the years of dieting when I gave up bread. Sometimes I'd have a banana sandwich if there were no decent vegetables. Most of the time, there were all kinds of foods on every menu that fit into my new ways.

My restaurant luck ended one night in New England on vacation with a tour. We were taken to a famous prime rib house that only had red meat, cheesy potatoes, garlic bread and french fried vegetables with apple pie for dessert. They didn't even have a slice of plain bread in the house so I ordered nothing but water. I felt peaceful with my choice to not eat and wasn't swayed by comments and questions from others in the group. I simply said, "I don't eat these foods but love being here talking with you." They quickly stopped bugging me (except for my husband who still couldn't get used to the new me) and accepted my few words of explanation. How different this was from the old days when others could pressure me. I used to offer long explanations to justify my food behavior, hoping to be accepted.

The hardest part about eating peacefully without obsession was remembering the highs of those peak moments of nirvana over a dessert or the buttered popcorn at the movies. I even missed some of the lows of those times when my behavior around food felt sinful. There was something delicious about shaking off the good girl and breaking all the rules for proper eating behavior.

It was a somewhat lonely time because I no longer felt like a kindred spirit when I led weight control groups. I used to avoid virtuous eaters and was scared that my students would no longer relate to me. My eating was based on deep values about my health without room for exceptions. The door to spurgeville was no longer on my pathway. I ate the same way day in and day out with no desire to deviate—not on vacation, not on my birthday, not on the weekend, not on holidays, not ever. I was totally consistent.

I missed being able to tell stories about my food challenges to my classes at Freedom From Fat. All my stories were from the past. People in my classes wanted to know how I was able to eat so healthfully and give up those foods I used to love but there was little to say. Something had happened deep inside that changed all my values around food and the demons that haunted my palate had disappeared. I was a happy food nerd.

A few months after the cancer, the earth moved big time as Los Angeles experienced a major earthquake that changed my residence and left me shaken way beyond the moments of the tremor. I was now face to face with the real big C—CONTROL! My weight problems and cancer taught me that I couldn't control my body. The earthquake let me know that I couldn't even control the ground under my feet. Everywhere I turned there was chaos from the broken buildings surrounding me to the panic of friends and clients who also lived in areas of the city close to the epicenter of the quake.

In my state of gratitude for my survival from both illness and natural disaster, I volunteered time counseling cancer patients and presenting workshops; meeting brave people, many of them very sick, who were seeking healing not just physically but on all levels of being. It was time to acknowledge what had always been there in the shadows of my life—the pull toward a deeper spiritual existence.

At the time of my cancer diagnosis, I was already in therapy and also using imagery for wellness on a regular basis. After the cancer diagnosis, I started seeing a gifted shamanistic healer and found a very spiritual acupuncturist in the same building as my counseling practice. I wanted caring guides to be with me as I embraced healing from the inside out.

I began to take long walks in nature and stare at the sky every night. Before going to bed, I would meditate in front of a candle and play tapes of New Age music. I started praying for people who were struggling with serious illness, along with general prayers for our earth and all who live on it. Some of the prayers were in my own words while others were in the Hebrew of my religious tradition. I not only deepened my connection to Judiasm but was also drawn to practices of Eastern traditions and those of the Native Americans.

My family didn't know what to make of this candle lighting, praying meditator who went out each night to communicate with the sky. Carol and Rob would roll their eyes and say, "Mom, you're sooooo spiritual," while supporting my efforts with presents of candles and all sorts of good luck tokens. I needed to go to extremes in order to catch up on all those years of pushing aside my deeper needs. The double whammy of cancer and earthquake got my attention in a way that could not be ignored. My spiritual practices gave me inner peace along with added energy to be there for others. I finally understood that old saying that one cannot give another water from an empty well.

It wasn't an accident that this period of inner growth came during the time that my eating was clean and wholesome. It would be great to report that my "zen" relationship to healthy food consumption lasted forever but that would be untrue. It was a magical time when my belief in healthy eating and my food consumption were one and the same. It lasted for five years and took me way beyond my recovery from cancer and crisis to years that were introspective and, at the same time, productive in the outer world.

I'm not quite sure what happened to end the "honeymoon." Maybe it was my mother's decline in her nineties when both eyesight and strength began to fail her. She was one of those gentle souls who was a therapist and philosopher by nature not schooling. Her message was constant and simple—that love was more important than anything else; that laughter brightens the dark and giving to others is as important as breathing. She was also someone who was able to eat lots of candy, ice cream and fatty food without any negative consequences in the way of major illness. In the last few years before her death, I'd visit her every day and began to slowly say yes to her offers of candy, delighting in her pleasure when she could give me a treat. She was no longer able to cook the chicken soup with vegetables that used to be her food gift to me.

Then there was a week long vacation in a small town where all the food was fried, processed or repulsive. Fruits and vegetables were either wilted, canned or absent altogether. The only appetizing items were desserts and I found myself suddenly wanting the cakes and cookies that for five years had been poison to me. The old me was back with a vengeance.

It didn't end when I got home to Los Angeles, the binge/diet capitol of the universe. It was the end of November, Thanksgiving, and I thrilled my family by baking my famous pumpkin cream pie, the one with fat grams as the main ingredient. No one missed the organic apple pie with whole wheat crust that I had brought to our holiday dinners for the past five years. Once again I was fighting with my brother over the turkey skin like we did as kids. Instead of feeling pleasantly satisfied at the end of the holiday meal, I could barely lift myself out of the chair.

Soon the food mania of December descended upon the country and I was back to my old routine of having the last supper all through the month ending with a big binge in preparation for a return to lean eating in the new year. The new year was 1998 and I was afraid that my feasting wouldn't stop until the new century, if ever.

Actually it took just a few months for me to get my bearings and reconnect with my support systems. I was no longer lecturing for any weight loss organizations but knew I could go back to a weight group as a member. I traded pumpkin pie for humble pie and started going to one of Dolly's Weight Watcher meetings on a weekly basis.

As I wiped off the crumbs from my fall back into old behavior, I was thrilled to find that my inner health nut was still alive and well. The daily wheatgrass drinking resumed as did the tofu burgers and organic produce. I wasn't eating red meat or bingeing big time and was still positively addicted to walking. Vitamin popping continued to replace jellybeans as my pills of choice. I was grateful for having had those five years to experience making good food choices from a deep sense of values without having to fight temptation and an endless wanting for too much of the wrong thing. My several weeks of junky eating receded into history.

Today, the dessert devil still tempts me but I don't sell my soul. I'm at peace with who I am in relation to food—someone who wants more than I choose to have but thoroughly enjoys what I do choose. The high/low cycle of eating is back but the highs are a little lower and the lows don't even approach bottom. Most of the time my eating is routine and healthy, but I don't take anything for granted.

When cancer struck, I wondered if I'd live long enough to see my young adult kids come into their full grown-up lives. Today, eight years later, my two children have become four as each has married wonderful partners. Now there are grandchildren, Jacob and baby Alice, two magical beings who own my heart.

Part of my spiritual journey has been a growing desire to leave a legacy and this book is one manifestation of that need. So much of my suffering and years of horrendous food habits could have been eased if I had a book like this in my life.

I hope that through this book you will be encouraged to let yourself be part of a holistic circle that surrounds you with health and sustenance, so you can live in ways that bring many blessings to you and those whose lives you touch.

This book is also my way of bringing you a wondrous present— the gift of my buddy and writing partner, Dolly. Dolly is one of those "earth-angels" who doesn't try to fix anyone but heals by the power of her loving presence and the magic of her stories. She is willing to open up her life and tell the whole world everything. She touches hundreds every week through her lectures. She is Lucy,

Mother Goose and the Good Witch from the Wizard of Oz all rolled up into one. Both of us hope this book will help you end the pain of the food-abuse/self-abuse cycle and live according to your dreams and values.

🦋 Dolly's Story

Food and I have a very complicated relationship going back as far as my memory, probably even further. The role of food in my life was born of a legacy handed down from my parents, rooted in their losses and struggle to stay alive during the horrors of the Holocaust. My deep connection to food is and has always been about survival, ritual, love, punishment, control, greed—every aspect of my being.

In my early years, there was too much—too much of high calorie greasy delicious Greek food meant to feed and console me through the difficult years of my childhood. I have always felt that when my mother nursed me, the milk that provided nourishment was also full of tears. When her eyes looked down at me as a baby, her vision was not focused on her firstborn child. She was seeing the ashes of her mother, father, sisters and brothers. I was taken care of physically but something was missing, some kind of connection. I couldn't feel my mother. I couldn't reach her.

I was born in Thessaloniki, Greece, in the middle of the turbulent twentieth century. This was the birthplace of my mother, father, and all the murdered ancestors who would have been my extended family.

My father was a prisoner in the death camps, while my mother fled from the Nazis. She and her brother and other fugitives hid underground in the mountains of Greece during the war. She told me many stories about how she lived with constant hunger and fear.

She trembled while telling of the night when the Nazis were walking on the ground just above where her group was hiding. One of the women was holding a baby who started crying. The father of the baby panicked and told his wife that she must shut the baby up or he would be forced to kill his own child. The cries were putting all of them in peril of being discovered. The mother silenced the baby by frantically feeding it from her breast until the cries subsided and everyone was safe for the moment. I learned that **food meant survival.**

Whenever there was no sign of Nazis around, my mother would go out and walk in the mountains to get some air. One day she came across an old rotten orange. She picked it up ever so gently and took it back to the hiding place, washed it and cooked it into a syrup that sustained her little group until the next source of food was found. I learned that **food was nourishment.**

My mother's hardships permeate my life even now, years after her death. If I throw away an overly ripe banana or a soft mushy orange, I hear my mother's voice whispering in my ear:

Dolly, that was so wasteful. You could have made banana bread like I did back in the days during the war. That orange could be boiled into syrup. Remember my story about my days in hiding when I found an orange and. . . .

I learned that **food was guilt.**

We came to America when I was three years old—war torn parents and a traumatized little Greek girl who was timid, scared and unable to speak a word of English.

Kindergarten took me from the protective cocoon of my home and threw me into a modern American setting where I really felt like the refugee child that I was. In my homemade clothes and funny hair style, I stood apart from the other children.

I was lonely and isolated and remember sitting alone at the school lunch bench eating. No one befriended the little girl who talked different, looked different, dressed different and ate strange food. My lunches consisted of homemade bread (before the days of trendy bread-maker machines), *feta* cheese, stuffed *filo* dough and yogurt that was made from scratch by my mom. Even though this food was odd to my classmates, it was familiar and delicious to me. **Food was my comfort, my solace.**

When I grew up and had kids of my own who happily went off to school each day, one of the questions that I always asked was, "Who did you have lunch with?" I just had to know that they were not sitting rejected on a bench somewhere off all alone.

Today, I'd love to have unique clothes expertly handmade for me. I wish I could still speak Greek fluently and indulge myself in endless lunches of homemade bread, *feta* cheese and *filo* dough pastries. Back then, all I wanted was to be part of the crowd—to fit in.

My early school years were a struggle as I was teased, laughed at, ostracized. I can remember looking forward to coming home, closing the door behind me at the end of a cruel day and being comforted by the sweet scent of the Greek foods my mom had been preparing all day. Eating them was even more comforting.

A ritual I shared with my mother was to sit in the living room devouring rich flaky *baklava* and drinking hot cocoa as we watched *The Secret Storm,* my mother's favorite soap opera. When I got older the hot cocoa became Turkish coffee and my mom would read the coffee grounds to tell me my future—when I would marry and how many children I was going to have. I loved those afternoons. **Food was intimacy, being with Mother. Food was love.**

Friday night was very sacred in our household. My mother would work all day in preparation for the evening when the Sabbath would begin at sundown. She would clean the house from top to bottom, then walk to the Greek grocery store to buy the cheese, *filo* dough, onions and olives for her filling pies, along with all the ingredients for the *baklava* dessert.

Our tradition was from the Sephardic (Spanish) roots of Judaism and our foods were not the typical gefilte fish, chicken soup and brisket of the Jews who came from Eastern Europe. We did enjoy the *challah* (twisted egg bread) that was a Sabbath staple in most Jewish homes. Sometimes our bulging table would include beans and homemade yogurt for dipping the rich bread. Our Sabbath meal was a feast—colorful, solid, substantial. I learned that **food was ritual. Food was holy.**

My parents struggled financially but always managed to keep us well fed. We would sit together as a family on those precious nights my father was not away at work. There were four of us, my mom, dad, me and my younger brother, Albert. If I didn't like the food put on my plate, I would have to sit until I ate it all. My parents reminded me over and over of the hardships behind that food. My dad worked so hard for the money that provided the meal. My mother slaved in the kitchen all day. There were still starving people everywhere. I would listen respectfully while hiding the eggs that I hated and gagging on the fish I couldn't stand. My personal food likes and dislikes didn't matter. I had to eat everything or sit at the table for hours. I learned that **food could be punishment.**

If I ate everything with enthusiasm, my parents were very pleased. I loved hearing "good for you" along with hugs and smiles. I learned that **food is a reward.**

During many years of my childhood, my dad worked two jobs. He labored at a factory during the day and worked at a bakery several nights. On those working nights, we would wait up for him until midnight when he would come home with hot fresh rolls. My mom would put a piece of chocolate in each steaming roll and as it melted we would sit around the kitchen table eating, as we welcomed my dad home and listened to his stories of the day. **Food was a reunion.**

I was the perfect kid in the family, leaving my poor brother the role of the unruly one who was constantly punished. My only vice was food, the good girl's drug of choice. In my family, I could never get in trouble for stuffing myself with food. My big appetite for my mother's cooking brought me praise. Her response to my request for another helping was always, "Good for you." I learned that **eating lots of food was being a good girl.**

As I left my young childhood and moved into my teen years when I had more freedom over my choices, those early food messages were deep in my psyche and set the scene for my ongoing misuse of food.

When I got my driver's license at 16, instead of cruising over to visit friends, I went to Jack-in-The-Box™ and ordered all the fun foods that never entered my home as a kid. I overdosed on fries, onion rings, hamburgers and milk shakes. I felt reborn behind the wheel of a car. Driving and eating fast food junk connected me to other typical American teens. I wasn't a foreigner anymore.

My good feelings didn't last long as I quickly learned that girls aren't supposed to have a hefty body or appetite. Secret eating became my preferred style. I was active in the theater scene during high school and loved playing parts, getting to be other people instead of me, having a healthy outlet for expressing emotion. There would be long afternoons rehearsing for plays with lots of breaks between scenes. I would hit the vending machine for candy, gum, mints—eating all my purchases unnoticed or so I thought.

There was this cute guy in my acting class who was the object of my romantic fantasies. He didn't seem to be aware of my existence until the afternoon he approached me during one of the breaks. I held my breath, waiting for him to flirt and then ask me for my phone number. I could barely contain myself as he started to speak, "Dolly, I've been watching you."

My heart was bursting with anticipation as he continued: "I notice that there is always something in your mouth. You're always chewing or eating something. Are you always hungry or just nervous?"

Suddenly, my vision of our future together disappeared, just like I wanted to do. I ran off, filled with embarrassment, muttering something about it being time for my scene rehearsal. I turned to food for comfort, even though it was food that had caused me such pain. This pleasure/pain relationship with food was to follow me for years to come.

My interest in both eating and acting continued as high school turned into college. My college degree was in Theater Arts. I also obtained a teaching credential so I would have a real way to earn money. Movie offers never poured in and teaching kids seemed like a wonderful thing to do. I felt such gratitude to those few teachers who sensed my early isolation and attempted to draw me into the group. I wanted to be someone who could make a difference to a child.

Soon I met my soulmate Alan, a young paramedic who was a real live hero in my eyes. He was also studying to be a chiropractor and seemed to have endless energy. He was open and friendly, filled with a zest for life. I wanted someone to rescue me and take me away. It was time for the shy little Greek girl to grow up, leaving behind my parents' Old World ways to begin my life as a modern young newlywed.

A year after our marriage, Aron was born. There are so many memorable moments surrounding the birth of a baby. Of course, one of mine was about food. I remember the delicious Chinese dinner we had just before I went into labor with as much detail as the labor itself. That was me, so connected to my feedings.

Three years later, our second son Robby was born. This was the pregnancy that brought me to my knees about my weight. A year after Robby's birth, I was carrying an extra fifty pounds on my short body and knew it was time to do something. I joined Weight Watchers. After trying to lose weight in so many unhealthy ways, I finally found a program that was right for me.

The meetings were totally engrossing. It blew me away to realize that the motivation for my eating was emotionally based. I was a very active participant in every meeting. After years of stuffing down my feelings, I had so much to say. Heads would nod in empathy as my torrent of words spilled out. After more than a year of slow but steady progress, the fifty pounds were off and I was at my goal weight.

My group leader at Weight Watchers wanted me to sign up for training to do what she was doing—lecturing and leading meetings. This wouldn't be acting. This would be the real me up there running meetings where people's lives were at stake, physically and emotionally. I was so nervous about that kind of challenge but she wouldn't take no for an answer.

Soon I was in training for a new career. This one would use both my theater skills and my background as a teacher. Working in the weight control industry would motivate me to stay at my weight goal and help others get where they wanted to be. It would also be a way to earn money and be a full time mother at the same time. Most of all, it would be the beginning of over twenty years of work with groups of people who let me be their inspiration just as they have been mine.

It was in Weight Watchers Training that I met Lynne—my friend, writing partner and a constant source of strength. We are kindred souls when it comes to eating challenges and support each other through the tough times. We are fulfilling a big dream by writing this book together.

My work as a lecturer for Weight Watchers was part time, allowing me to focus on my family. My sons were getting bigger and I longed for one more child. I had two miscarriages in the past and knew my chances of having a third child were not great, but fate smiled down on my family and our daughter Katie was born. I vowed to raise her to be at peace around food and proud of her body. That promise has been quite a challenge in a culture that is so unsupportive of positive body image.

My adult life was a whirlwind as I kept working, raising my children, trying to be a source of support for my increasingly busy husband. Alan had planned on retiring early from being a paramedic to work full time as a chiropractor. Instead, he was promoted to Chief of Paramedics and became head of emergency services for the Los Angeles Fire Department. He was constantly on call through an eventful period of several years that included riots, fires, floods and even a major earthquake. As his responsibilities multiplied, so did mine. It was hard not to turn to food for an emotional lifeline. That's when I would return to Weight Watchers as a member so I could get back to goal weight and continue my work as a lecturer.

Throughout those times of weight fluctuations, my major eating was in the closet. My children never saw me eat in their young years, especially the boys. If the FBI had taken my sons in for cross examination, put bright lights on them, and questioned them relentlessly asking: "Why does your mother have a weight problem, Why, why, why? What does she eat?" They would only be able to shake their heads and say, "We don't know. We never see her eat."

It took reading, support groups and intensive therapy for me to realize how food was my drug, the ideal substance for a good girl who would never do anything shady. Food was appropriate, acceptable and legal. Food was fun and fun was food.

My emotional struggles around eating got more complex after the fifty pounds came off. I had lost weight, made wonderful behavior changes, become a popular lecturer but was still stuck in some of my old patterns. I was scared and confused even during some of the moments of lecturing to an overflowing room of people, sharing tears and laughter, desperately wanting to be worthy of their trust in me as a role model.

I finally came to accept that losing weight was a beginning, not an ending. If food and the compulsive behavior around it was my addiction, then I needed to work on my "sobriety" every day. This was going to be a slow process, a baby step at a time and the time would be as long as it takes.

In the process of losing weight, I learned how to order salad dressing on the side, drink water, take walks, and broil fish; but I didn't know how to handle my feelings, voids, and challenges without eating. I was and still can be an emotional eater. I ate to soothe myself and numb my yearning, longing, needing, wanting. When I ate, I did not feel anger, sorrow or fear. I also did not get to feel joy other than the momentary pleasure of the food fix. I wanted to eat all the time. When I curtailed my eating, I felt deprived and ate over those feelings.

I understand today how my life has been interwoven with the early messages that shaped me. Food has been my way to feel connected. It gets inside me and I'm no longer alone. I'm full. Hunger and deprivation feel like death—dark, lonely, despairing. The opposite of death is life. Feeling full is to feel full of life, to triumph over the threat of extinction that my father faced in the death camp where he lost everyone including a wife and baby girl; to triumph over the hunger that my mother felt as she lived on the adrenaline of fear along with meager supplies. Feeling full is an illusion of comfort that had to go in order for me to fill my adult life with the satisfying choices of marriage, kids and work that provide more nourishment than a binge from the local Greek deli.

There's a popular children's book by P.D. Eastman called *Are You My Mother?* It's a story about a little baby bird waking up in his nest alone when his mother left to find him food. The baby feels scared, confused, abandoned—deprived of mommy.

He leaves the tree in search of his mother. He sees a dog and asks, "Are you my mother?"

The answer, of course, is, "No."

He goes to other animals looking for mother and then to inanimate objects. He wonders if the bulldozer or boat is his mother. Finally, he finds his true mother and is happy once more.

I often feel like that baby bird. I'm looking for my mommy even though she is dead now. I've always been looking for her, even when she was holding me, feeding me from her body with those tearful eyes.

I looked for my mommy in food. I asked the chocolate chip cookies, "Are you my mommy?" I didn't realize the answer was "no" until the box was totally consumed. I went to the pizza, candy, ice cream—especially the soft sweet ice cream like mother's milk. I would turn to many varieties of foods but none of them were my mother. I never felt full. When turning to food for emotional sustenance, I would eat and feel nothing other than a momentary reprieve from the emptiness.

My quest to understand how my past has impacted my present has been a journey toward a more compassionate existence. I have found my mother and also my father. My willingness to look at the painful history of my war-torn family connected me to some very uplifting memories. My parents were filled with anger, fear and sorrow but nothing could extinguish the light within them. Today I can appreciate the blessings of their unbelievable spirit.

My mother was a very good storyteller and had a great sense of humor. She continually kept her friends smiling and laughing. She would cook wonderful delicacies and sing Greek songs to keep their spirits up. My parents were part of a community of Greek Holocaust survivors who had suffered so many losses and years of unspeakable horrors. She was the one they turned to for inspiration.

Even in those outcast young elementary school years, I used what I learned from my mother and began to make the other kids laugh with me not just at me. There were some good times when my own stories and jokes helped jump start my long journey toward belonging. Today, in both my lecturing and counseling, humor and stories are part of who I am. Students and clients tell me how much that personal way of connecting touches them. It is hard to accept that people love me for my vulnerable places.

My mother was open to many ways of healing outside of traditional medicine. She had a homeopathic cure for everything including some practices that may seem very strange today. She was a master at "cupping" or *"Venduza"* as it was called in Greece, a technique to relieve back pain or discomfort in other body parts by putting glass cups on the affected area. Fire was used to remove the air in the cups, creating a vacuum. It was like a more civilized version of using leeches to suck out the poisons. By the age of ten, I was quite skilled in all types of ancient medical treatment for numerous maladies. That early "doctoring" gave me the open mind I have today when working with people with weight problems who feel hopeless because they have "tried everything." I'm totally open to all kinds of ways to heal and learned very young to embrace a holistic way of being.

My mother was very free and open with her body even though she walked with a limp. She ate what she wanted, gained weight beyond what was considered normal in American culture, but never got into yo yo weight fluctuation. She never weighed herself or said anything negative about her size. I gave my daughter my mom's name, Katie, with the hope that she would be filled with the best of my mother, including a comfortable relationship with her body.

My legacy of tears spawned in me a sense of joy and gratitude for being alive. I draw from the well of strength that my family gave me in times of struggle. My optimism is boundless. I'm able to reframe almost any situation so that it is manageable.

My parents gave me the instinctual ability to survive and today I fully embrace my good life filled with family, friends and meaningful work. I'm now a psychotherapist in private practice as well as a lecturer for Weight Watchers. I don't know of any greater joy than to be able to touch lives in a meaningful way and be touched back.

Humor is the staff of life—the bread of my existence that allows me to rise above almost any situation even if only momentary. I laugh at myself and poke fun at my little kid ways from a place of compassion that draws others to me. My daily diet of laughter and love soothes my hunger. I finally know what it means to be full.

This book is a way of sharing with you what I have learned in my journey toward living in the land of plenty where feasting can be as painful as starving, where too much can trigger old feelings of not enough. My wish is to help you rise above the circumstances that have put you in the food-abuse/self-abuse cycle so you can move with compassion in the direction of your deepest dreams.

 # Closing

We believe that this is not the end but the beginning of a time of positive change for you. Take an action now to begin the process of release from the grip of the food-abuse/self-abuse cycle.

We hope we have touched your lives and given you information, encouragement and inspiration so you can fulfill the desire for transformation that you felt when you picked up this book. We are rooting for you.

Dolly Cowen

Lynne Goldklang

Notes:

Order Extra Copies for Your Friends and Family.

Count It As A Vegetable . . . and Move On! is an important book for anyone struggling with food abuse and/or self-abuse problems. It might just make the difference for someone you love.

Cost is $14.95 per copy.

Add $2.00 for postage and handling for the first copy and $1.00 for each additional copy to be shipped to the same address.

Send check or money order, along with your name, address and zip code to:

The Nurturing Connection
5923 Kanan Road
Agoura Hills, CA 91301

(818) 725-3125

Allow three weeks for delivery